Unconditional Love

SUCKS!

How an Old Myth Ruins Relationships

J. A. Dougherty

© Copyright 2019, 2024
ISBN: 9781090499882
All rights reserved.

Early Reviews

"If you've ever been in a relationship where you felt you were always holding the short end of the stick, check out this book. From the five, on-point strategies for relationship success (they're not what you're thinking), to the hilarious examples, this book educates and simultaneously entertains."

—Kelli Maw, MD, physician and author

"Whether you believe in unconditional love or not, Dougherty's academic pedigree, expertise in wealth management, and long-term experience advising couples contribute to the creation of a book that is a must-read for singles or those embarking on a serious relationship. He draws on recognizable celebrities and movies as exemplars for his key points in entertaining ways. However, don't be fooled. The useful questionnaires, checklists, and advice included in the book should be taken seriously."

—Dr. Kay Stahl, Clinical Professor, NYU

"I was one of those people who thought I believed in unconditional love in a romantic relationship. This book has convinced me otherwise. In addition, the author presents a plethora of sound, practical advice that will help anyone make better choices in their mate and help those of us who are already in a relationship make it work better."

—Michael E. Angier, author, Life Coach

*"*Unconditional Love SUCKS! *provides great advice for those contemplating a serious relationship or marriage. Dougherty has even included several questionnaires to help guide you. I recommend it to persons in the dating game and newlyweds alike, who can still work on and agree on what you want, what you expect, what you can change, and what you will change to help ensure that you can be in one of those wonderful relationships that live unconditional love."*

—Robert J. Schneider, M.A., Ph.D, Psychologist

"As a CPA with a busy practice, I wish I had copies of this book in years past that I could have handed out to several of my clients struggling with relationship issues. It would have saved all of us a lot of time, effort, and paperwork in trying to sort problems. I'll definitely keep some copies in my waiting room."

—David W. Ormiston, CPA, M.A.

Table of Contents

Introduction 1
Part One 7
I LOVE YOU UNCONDITIONALLY – NOW HERE'S WHAT I EXPECT 7
Chapter 1 Conditions for Unconditional Love 9
Chapter 2 Expectations are a Bitch 17
Chapter 3 Can You Pass This Test of a Million Tiny Conditions? 29
Part Two CREATING THE RIGHT CONDITIONS FOR LOVE SUCCESS 39
Chapter 4 Forget Gypsy Psychics—Your Lover's Parents Predict the Future 41
Chapter 5 Falling for Successful and Beautiful People—the Ugly Realities 57
Chapter 6 Every Action Gets a Reaction—in Love, Too 67
Chapter 7 The Sex Chapter 83
Chapter 8 The Money Chapter *Or* One Bed, Two Banks 93
Chapter 9 Modern Men, Women, and Other Genders 107
Part Three PERSONALITY STYLES—SOME CONDITIONS ARE UNCONDITIONAL 123
Chapter 10 Predictable Behaviors You'll Be Stuck With 125
Chapter 11 Detecting Personality Styles Outside the Bedroom 159
Part Four THE LEGAL FRAMEWORK FOR ROMANCE – IN A CONDITIONAL WORLD 171
Chapter 12 Divorce: A Beginning, Not and Ending 173
Chapter 13 A New Framework: The Promise Marriage 183
Chapter 14 Because I Want You 193
An Important Request 197
Thank You Notes 198
Photo Credits and Licenses 199
About the Author 200

Introduction

In real life, would the characters of Richard Gere and Julia Roberts in *Pretty Woman* still be happy, even three months after the wedding?

In *You've Got Mail*, do we really believe Tom Hanks and Meg Ryan will start being nice after hating each other for 95% of the movie?

In the fantasy land of Hollywood, we see romantic couples with serious flaws fight like dogs in the beginning, but eventually fall in love, and live—we are led to believe—happily ever after.

We accept this myth because it relies on another: unconditional romantic love.

Everyone advises us to practice unconditional love with our partner so we can get through rough times and disappointments. After our break-up, however, it becomes an unexplained missing ingredient in our desperate attempt to figure out what the hell really happened.

Breaking the Hollywood Myths

We'll discuss why unconditional romantic love is a myth and why a *conditional* love works better, and what you have to do to make it work. Did you ever ask yourself why it is that when we are dating, we tell ourselves—and all our friends and parents remind us, too—that before we commit to a relationship, we should be sure that our lover is good enough for us. In essence, the new lover has to satisfy a level of expectations that we justifiably have. Yes, even if we don't admit it, we have a checklist of conditions that we would like to see in our new love interest. And if we internet date, it is obvious in the first questionnaire we complete.

But then magically, after we say our "I dos" at the alter, we are told to declare that our love has *no* conditions. Really?

I suspect you're reading this book because you just met the love of your life. Or you want to meet the love of your life. Or, you're having problems with someone you want to be the love of your life.

As you embark on your love voyage, consider five new strategies that may blow your mind but will make for a better romance:

1. Do not count on unconditional love as a path for success.
2. Each partner should evaluate and communicate their <u>true</u> objectives and expectations in the relationship.
3. Don't count on your partner to change—at least for the better.
4. Be careful when commingling financial assets—or debt or expenses—with your partner, even after moving in together or marriage.
5. If doubtful of conventional marriage, consider a love bond other than legal marriage. It may save the relationship and certainly the romance.

The Nuts and Bolts of Love Success

We all have to admit that, by default, half of the hang-ups in any relationship are our own. Even though this book attempts to create predictability about a relationship, we cannot predict the problems that we ourselves bring. Why? Because, for the most part, we deny the problems that we have. But hey, ignoring our shortcomings probably helps many of us to go out into the world every day and have some kind of confidence to function with others. I would estimate that 90% of the people that talk to me say it is the fault of the other person for a breakup or divorce, even if the person telling me this has an addiction problem, cheated, or beat his or her spouse. Go figure.

Instead of predictably chasing the beautiful or ultra-successful person, what should you really look for? We'll talk about why many of the dating sites out there may be barking up the wrong tree and how to better assess your search results. You'll also read how to expect less instead of more in a relationship and be happier for it. I will reveal why only 25% of couples have good sex lives—at least with each other. We'll discuss how you can predict your own happiness or misery in a relationship based on patterns of behavior that you will be able to classify shortly after meeting that dreamboat. Of course, I can't end without telling you how to manage your finances to achieve eternal bliss.

The conventional wisdom also instructs us to just get along with our in-laws and accept them for what they are. I'm going to tell you how to evaluate them to understand what lies in store for your own future.

And speaking of the future, as women find new opportunities in leadership and career fields, you might believe everything is coming up roses for relationships. But both men and women with whom I work in this new era are finding patches of dead flowers.

We've approached an era in which the woman in a relationship often earns more money than the man, has a better job with more authority, frequently leaving him confused and intimidated. If you think this is overstated, realize that many colleges in the United States have almost twice as many female as male students. If we don't think all this has ramifications for relationships, money, and the future, we're being blindly naive.

Aah, the challenges.

Many of the approaches I advocate appear to be contrarian behaviors, set to turn romance upside down. But let's face it, if all the myths of romance were true, we would not have an almost 50% divorce rate and the lowest marriage trend among young people since they started keeping records. Indeed, the internet speed-dating phenomenon structurally helps many participants avoid relationships entirely. If all that weren't scary enough, more than 40% of American babies today are born to unwed mothers.

Honeybun, Can You Scratch that Itch I Can't Seem to Reach?

There's another old movie called *The Seven Year Itch*. The premise is that after about seven years of marriage for humans, one of the mates gets restless and starts looking for other animals in the jungle.

But, in my professional experience, as a financial planner and counselor, if a marriage is really a disaster, it won't go much more than two years. The ceremony at the Elvis chapel in Vegas was fun, but after everybody sobered up, they asked themselves what the hell they were thinking.

At the other end of the time spectrum, statistics show more and more divorcing after slugging it out over a longer period: 25% of all divorces now comprise people over the age of 50. Relationships spanning longer than 20 years allow plenty of time for the partners to really know each other's strengths and weaknesses, and to raise children to young adulthood. During this time, they've also had time to go into debt, fight, be tempted by a good-looking co-worker, and eventually come to be sick of each other. After all this, they may indeed be ready to move on to other mates in the wild. But, should that be all we can really expect—a bumpy 20 years—if we're lucky?

I've seen people get divorced after 45 days; I've seen others get divorced after 45 years. Why that person needed a new boyfriend after almost five decades is something I may never figure out. One lady told me she should have left her husband 30 years earlier. Knowing her husband pretty well myself, she was probably right.

My job as a financial counselor, to rich and poor, young and old, allows me to observe couples over many, many years. There is a startling pattern that I've witnessed which shows that those individuals who seem to be emotionally abused in the relationship die first. I swear, it's almost as if they are willing to take the ultimate escape route to get out of their lousy marriage. So you see, this book is really about someone's life and death—yours.

Heaven Can Wait

The following pages embark on a mission to disclose what types of behaviors make for a successful long-term relationship. I hope to open the reader's eyes as to what they—what all of us—are getting into when we look for love in all the right, and wrong, places. And, happy partnerships don't come about without happy passion, and vice versa. As Big Mamma told her daughter-in-law in the play, *Cat on a Hot Tin Roof*. "When a marriage goes on the rocks, the rocks are here," slapping her hand on the big brass bed.

Often, that which we expect from romantic love never really happens. We have our own plans, our own objectives. Frequently, we couch the idea of love in the other things we want out of life.

You've heard the phrase, everybody wants to go to heaven, but nobody wants to die. Similarly, everybody wants a long-term romance, but nobody wants its boredom. Or pain. Or work. Or all the other crap. So, are we doomed from the start?

NO!

Read on.

One note before we start: Throughout the reading, I may refer to husbands, wives, men, women, etc., but the reader should realize that these roles today commonly shift among *all* of us—female-male, straight-gay, and everything in between. Adjust as needed to the character of the person I tag. Also, you may tire of seeing the interchangeable use of gender pronouns, he/she, her/him. Frequently I will simply use the new gender-neutral substitute pronouns, they/them. I apologize to my editor in advance.

Aah, the challenges indeed.

Part One

I LOVE YOU UNCONDITIONALLY – NOW HERE'S WHAT I EXPECT

Chapter 1
Conditions for Unconditional Love

Dick: "Cut off my ears, steal my money, and I'll love you anyway?"
Grace: "Yes—and more."
—Movie, *Unconditional Love*, 2002

We hear it on television; we see it on greeting cards. We especially include it in our wedding vows: I love you unconditionally; we must have unconditional love. Will you stay with me unconditionally?

Remember this: Romantic love comes with conditions, and believing it does not, will doom your relationship.

Unconditional Failures

My spouse and I recently attended a dinner party with three married couples. When the conversation turned to unconditional love, they all asserted to believe it to be one of the most important precepts of marriage. Absolutely and without a doubt.

But wait a minute, I said, as I looked around the table. *You* have been divorced once, and *you* have been divorced twice, and *you* have been divorced twice—at least. And I'm not in my first marriage, either. If unconditional love exists, why aren't we all still with our first spouses, and for that matter, our first true loves?

Well, one woman responded, her husband had an affair. I asked her why she didn't forgive him and stay. Another person at the table said that his spouse suffered chronic alcohol addiction. I asked why he didn't hang in there and try to get her help. Yet another admitted she fell in love with a successful office worker. How would that be? After all, I asked, wasn't the love for your *spouse* unconditional?

In short, if unconditional love, or what I refer to as UL, really existed for partners, there would be no divorce. We would ride through the storms of marriage and just hang in there. The fact that we have an almost 50% divorce rate tells me that half of our marital couples found *conditions* that they, in fact, could *not* tolerate.

Do the other 50% who remain married simply suffer eternally? No, of course not . . . one of the spouses eventually dies.

Serial Killer Children are the Exception

The closest we come to UL is with parent and child, but that is the extent of it. Yes, your children may be drug dealers, child molesters, or worse, members of the opposing political party, but you will still find it in your heart to love them. We've all seen it: The parents of a murderer on the evening news lament about their child's heinous actions, but near the end of the interview, they so often say that their adult daughter was just under stress when she drowned her three kids. Or they say that their son is really a good boy—he just had a mental problem when he gunned down everyone in the restaurant. And they confirm their love for the murdering son, even after he is led to the electric chair.

We also see unconditional love *from* a child to parent, even when the child may have been abused. Parents can make wickedly nasty and hurtful comments. And they may be physically abusive. At the end of the day, or year, or lifetime, the child often still loves the parent. Hell, I still love my parents even after they exposed me to secondhand cigar smoke and put me in a car without seat belts.

The unconditional love that a parent has for his or her child is a mysterious biological factor that is wonderful to see in humans and other species. It helps us raise the child through times of turmoil, mistakes, and failure. We are there for the child no matter their shortcomings. We forgive them and continue to love.

Yes, I have seen parents who are cold to their children and even cruel. But I believe that is the exception and not the rule to the basic biology of raising a child—whether you're a celebrity in L.A. or an elephant in the jungle.

Most remarkably, we also witness unconditional love with our pets, even though, let's face it, it is more their unconditional love for us. Our dog has few expectations except that we feed him and take him for a walk. But would even faithful Max love us if we didn't do these basic chores?

There's an old joke that a dog is better than a lover because if you locked your mate in the trunk of a car for three hours, and then opened the trunk to let them out, they'd want to smash your head against the bumper. On the other hand, if you freed your *dog* from the same trunk, he'd wag his tail and lick your face. Now that's unconditional love.

If you learn nothing else from these chapters, learn what I have observed over the years: In romantic relationships, UL does not exist. And, even if successful couples don't advertise it and probably deny it if asked, the best relationships know that you should not rely on the myth of unconditional love.

Rather than a cure for problems, the premise of unconditional love in romance often creates a slow terminal death in the relationship. As soon as we get into a relationship and fall back on the assumption of unconditional love, we often stop trying to keep the relationship good and making it better. The cliché is true: We take each other for granted. More accurately: We take our *situation* for granted.

He thinks, "Why should I have to bring you flowers anymore? You're supposed to love me unconditionally, whether I get the damn flowers or not. Too bad for you if I lay here on my fat ass and watch the football game all day. What can you do about it—you're *supposed* to love me—unconditionally." Or, "I know I had an affair with my hunky co-worker, but I am counting on your unconditional love for forgiveness. Remember, you told me you'll love me unconditionally as you recited those words to the world and we held hands at the altar." These are stated in exaggerated terms, but the essence becomes all too true.

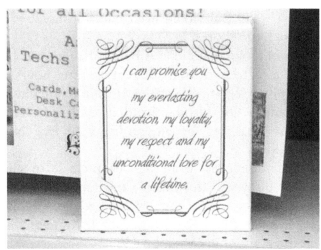

Sweet Promises to hang on your wall as seen for sale in a stationery store. None of my divorced friends remembered buying such a card.

And if that's not enough, we all watch *The Bachelor* reality TV show. Unconditional love is all they ever talk—and dream—about. In fact, it's a requirement—in addition to everyone having a really nice ass.

The Maid Having Your Husband's Baby is Not Acceptable

I'm sure Maria Shriver thought her love was unconditional for celebrity Arnold Schwarzenegger—obviously, he did, too. Who has been more successful than this guy? Isn't it natural, then, he would assume wife Maria would accept such a man unconditionally and overlook his faults? He was Mr. Olympia an incredible seven times, a mega movie star, two-term governor, and zillionaire. With all these qualities, wouldn't it be easy—or at least easier—for wife Maria to put his historical dalliances in the past and forgive him of any weaknesses—unconditionally? That is, before he had a child with the house maid. Just ask her divorce attorney if you think Maria now believes in UL. Maria calls Arnold *The Terminator* for another reason these days.

And you would think it doesn't get any more unconditional than with the situation of Brad Pitt and Angelina Jolie. Six lovely kids, endless palatial estates, and millions of dollars to kick around. You would kinda' think that near the beginning of their relationship they would have said to each other, "Honey, we don't want to lose all this by having some kind of crazy conditions or terms, so let's make absolutely sure we have a love that is unconditional." Whoops. It looks like somebody had conditions.

Alas, we come to Hillary Clinton. (We will often.) You tell me that she's still with Bill—at this writing, anyway. There's a lot of water under their bridge. He has had numerous affairs. Who knows, perhaps she has, too. Many individual successes and failures have crossed their paths during the couple's tumultuous lives. Do you really believe they have the same type of love they had 35 years ago? If you do, then perhaps you still believe in unconditional love.

Instead, let's look at the Clintons another way. Perhaps they are still together because Bill and Hillary have a very *conditional* relationship, in which there are very specific terms and understandings that allow them each to function together according to these implicit or perhaps even explicit terms. If true, their relationship may be a better illustration of conditional rather than unconditional love, whether or not you agree with the terms they've accepted. It works for them; they may indeed have a deep love for each other. And for these reasons, I have a curious respect for what they have.

Hollywood Romance, Unconditional Love Style

Speaking of celebrity couples, be careful not to be misled by what you see in Hollywood movies. In every romantic comedy, we initially see couples having a conflict, and often one of them even starts out as a jerk. Then, magically, the jerkiness wears off, and the jerk realizes he loves her, and she realizes she loves him, and by the end of the movie, they are happily together. This is the age-old formula.

In real life, however, it is a formula for disaster.

What we don't see is the sequel. If Part One of the movie is titled *True Love on Elm Street*, Part Two is titled *Nightmare on Elm Street*. In Part Two, the couple are miserable because he went back to being a jerk. Did you ever notice that we don't see a lot of sequels with romantic comedies? Ever wonder why?

Real life is not like a Hollywood Romantic Comedy!

In real life, we hope everyone is supposed to be nice to each other when they're dating—not just after they've tied the knot. And, unlike Hollywood characters, if one of the partners is a jerk in the beginning, you can bet your life—or future happiness—they will be an obnoxious jerk later. They *aren't* going to get any better after you are committed to each other. Not after you move in together, not after you lease a car together, not after you get married—and certainly not after you have children together. Please read this paragraph at least once more.

Jovial or Jerk?

Should we take a minute to define a jerk? It includes any behavior or disagreement that makes a person—male or female—unpleasant to be with. And, in relationships, a disagreement can sink to the classification of jerkiness sooner than you think. Anything that you and your partner decisively disagreed with on the relationship test you'll see later in Chapter 3 can eventually make your partner a jerk. I know that a failed self-test might sound too black and white, but it is not. That which is a disagreement now (such as, "I want to go out with friends, but my girlfriend says she's sad because she wants me all to herself tonight—God, she's so sweet!") morphs into a major problem two years down the road ("My bitchy wife won't let me go to Vegas with my buddies, but screw her, I'm going anyway!")

If you think that living together or marriage will make the jerkiness melt away, dream on.

Many of us have seen the popular movie with Jack Nicholson and Helen Hunt, *As Good As it Gets*. Nicholson plays a talented but troubled obsessive-compulsive bachelor, who we see in the movie regularly visiting his shrink. Nobody in society can deal with his rude behavior, as illustrated by the diner he regularly visits. He yells, is abusive to a waitress, and insults his neighbors. Over the course of the movie, he develops a relationship with the waitress, played by Helen Hunt, and they gradually fall in love. And by the end of the movie, they are together, though he continues to struggle with his mental health. In the movie, when asked by the waitress played

Unconditional Love Sucks!

by Hunt for a compliment, he tells her, "You make me want to be a better man." Ah, that's so loving; she's touched, and we are, too. By the end of the movie they are together and ostensibly happy.

I would love to see the sequel to this movie, in which he resumes being a jerk. I suppose the audience and the waitress want to forgive Nicholson's character because he has the very unlikely talents for writing tender romance novels and playing a beautiful piano, in addition to using some of his wonderful wealth to pay medical expenses for Hunt's son. In this way, the screenwriter manipulates us into believing that these skills reveal a kind soul that encourage us to want to live with him, and because of this underlying talent, we can forgive all the mental illness and obnoxiousness—and continue to love him unconditionally.

However, in real life, we really couldn't put up with his shit, but we don't want to tell ourselves that when we're dating him—and driving in his (or her) new sports car.

In real life, when starting a romance, we look past all the problems that are visible, and somehow think that deep down, because the other person has money, or was nice to us on a date, or gave us good sex, we can forgive, and live with, this jerk. In addition to allowing a Hollywood writer to manipulate our feelings, we also allow ourselves to manipulate illusions of what we are getting into.

And so, in the realistic film sequel I would create for Nicholson and Hunt, the marriage lasts six months. She is back waiting on tables, and he's back alone in his apartment, playing the piano—with no one to listen.

Another Hollywood version of jerk-to-jovial is *You've Got Mail*. You know, the one with Meg Ryan and Tom Hanks. I know more than a few people who tell me it's one of their all-time favorites. In case you are one of the few on the planet who have not seen it, the film is about two people who send each other emails without identifying themselves, and through the emails, they are best of friends and very gushy. By chance, they happen to know each other in real life, too, but they don't know that the other is their email correspondent. In their *real-life* relationship, they *hate* each other, antagonize each other, and, let's face it, are *both* jerks.

Ah, but by the end of the movie, however, you guessed it. They discover each other's email secret and walk hand-in-hand off into the sunset—in a beautifully flowered park, no less. Their earlier meanness and uncivility have ceased, because, apparently, the sole reason for their meanness, and being a jerk, was only because they thought they *should* have been jerks—at the time. But now they can see that their email partners are really each other, and the real people are pretty cool. And magically and suddenly, they stop being mean, vindictive people.

The myth of UL we read about goes back hundreds of years. Jane Austin's novel *Pride and Prejudice* was a work of genius in how she managed to create a slow romantic burn between the two main characters, Elizabeth Bennet and Mr. Darcy. Through misunderstandings and prejudgments (alright, call it pride and prejudice), the two love interests are miserable with each other through most of the story. At the end, however, they miraculously break through all this crap and live happily ever after. We read this, and we tell ourselves, if they can do it, we can, too.

But we can't. If we are miserable with each other while dating, with fights, misunderstandings, frustrations, and jerkiness, we are going to be even more miserable after a commitment of marriage, children, and credit card debt. Only in make-believe can partners not like each other at first, exhibit terrible flaws, but then, by the end of the story, live happily ever after.

At their root, these stories have a common theme: the premise that the lovers do not like each other at first, as if something is impeding their correct view of each other. And later, as the plot continues, this impediment disappears; they suddenly realize their former behavior wasn't really their true behavior, which allows them to fall in love—unconditionally.

The whole idea of the myth is that unconditional love does exist and because it exists, it allows us to overlook the other person's problems. We therefore temporarily suspend our own conditions of happiness, allowing us to believe in a blissful future.

Is life a romantic comedy? Statistics of divorce and unwed parents indicate otherwise. But maybe we can have a happy ending, anyway. Read on.

Chapter 2
Expectations are a Bitch

"Ask no questions, and you'll be told no lies."
—*Great Expectations,* Charles Dickens

One of the reasons that an adult can love a child unconditionally is that the adult normally has very little *expectation* of receiving anything from the child during the child's development stage. We do not expect our children to pay us for services rendered, as nice as that sounds, or for the child to feed or nurture us—at least not before we are back to using diapers ourselves. We expect to do all the giving.

Although parents may get frustrated with their children, it usually doesn't end the relationship. I agree that parents may expect their children to get good grades and marry the right person—and get a job. But the parent expects that for the *child's* benefit, not their own.

When we are in a romantic relationship, it is entirely different. Our expectations—what we expect—of the other is not for the other's benefit, but for *our* benefit. We expect the other person, our lover, to give *us* compliments, have sex with us, go out to the movies with *us*, to look nice for *us*, and of course, to be faithful to *us*. When those expectations—those conditions—are not met, our love will probably wane. I know that sounds potentially heretical, but it's true.

Don't confuse child-parent love with romantic love.
It's a set-up for failure.

Are you beginning to understand that the expectations factor is the most important part of a romantic relationship? When our expectations are met, we are happy, we're in love. Even if those we have created in our mind turn out to be destructive later. As long as we believe that we are getting from the other party what we want, we are satisfied.

When expectations are not satisfied by either mate, the relationship starts to crumble. So, it's very important to identify what you expect from the other person.

Is that a Lawyer—or Just His Car—that I'm in Love With?

Most times we go into a relationship with what I call the expectation mirage. We think we are in love with the other person. If he is a successful attorney or celebrity, are we not really in love with him as much as with his status or income he—or she—may provide?

In an interview once, movie star Leonardo DiCaprio said his love life was a mess because he could never believe a female's expression of love for him. He was always afraid that her quest for his fame and money blinded the woman—her expectation mirage—from getting to know Leonardo the person rather than the mega star of *Titanic*. Nevertheless, you may take heart, young ladies, because, as of this writing, he continues to date beautiful actresses and models, who clearly have an expectation of raising their own celebrity status by associating with him.

As it turns out, perhaps one of these beauties did not have her expectations met when she reacted by hitting Leonardo over the head with a broken bottle. She received a jail term of two years. I don't know if DiCaprio visited her while she was incarcerated.

Why do you think it is that celebrities so often fall in love with other celebrities? Why don't you see the stars falling in love with the lighting director or the cameraman or, God forbid, their financial advisor? The lighting director could turn out to be much better in the sack than Leonardo. And we know the financial planner would probably be very good at managing the star's money. Why do celebrities go right past all these wonderful people and head straight for the other nutty movie star? Because that is not what their objective really is. They're viewing their own expectations and probably have more than one expectation mirage themselves.

Low Expectations = High Fun

When guys are teenagers, we know that a fancy car driving down Main Street will impress the ladies. As we get older, we know a fancy job or title will impress the ladies. For the ladies, they know that looking good will impress the men. By looking good, they are satisfying our expectation that we want somebody who is attractive. We naturally have told ourselves that a good-looking partner is something we *expect* in a relationship.

If you really want to see the impact that expectations have on a relationship, here are a few illustrations. Let's start with when you are first dating. When you are first dating, you have *no* expectation of each other, other than primarily appearance. You don't expect the other person to work to put bread on your table, you don't expect them to pay the bills for you, and you don't expect them to take care of your child—yet. You simply go out for dinner and enjoy a movie, and if things are going well, maybe have different degrees of sex.

Expectations are very low at this point in the relationship, and therefore happiness is very high. There is an inverse relationship between expectations and happiness. That is, the lower the expectations are, the higher the happiness in a relationship, and vice versa.

The Lower Expectations are, the Higher the Happiness is.

Another example of low expectations and high happiness happens when two people have an adulterous affair. What do you expect of your lover? Not much, really. Just show up at the hotel in the afternoon and have sex. That's it. The lovers don't expect each other to make sure the electric bill is paid or that the kids' braces get adjusted. They don't even expect a nice gift for Christmas—maybe. The expectation is very limited, very focused. Show up, have good sex, and go home. When the lovers are cocooned in the Holiday Inn, it's unlikely the conversation turns to the kids' braces.

What can we learn from the adulterous affair? Simply, if we lower our expectations, we can increase our happiness.

But what do we really mean when we say expectations? Expectations are conditions—conditions of the relationship. We all have conditions, and that is not necessarily bad. Realizing that conditions exist prepare us to be a better partner. And, because conditions are a reality, the partners have to continually satisfy the others' conditions and expectations for there to be success. Yes, you must satisfy your partner's expectations to keep them happy. Or, put another way, they will be satisfied if their expectations are met.

You may be wondering at this point: "Are you telling me I have to find a person who either has low expectations, especially if I'm not bringing much to the party myself? And, do I have to find a person who has identified what their expectations are, and then I have to determine if I can satisfy these expectations?"

Yes, and that's not the worst of it. We can't forget that the job of meeting expectations is a continuous task. We have to continue to bring home flowers, look forward to having wild sex, and perhaps keep that pain-in-the-ass job that we would love to quit.

When expectations are not met, the relationship goes downhill fast, and often we find the change in tone of the lovers dramatically reversed. It fascinates me when the television gossip show, Hollywood Insider reports a celebrity break-up like Johnny Depp and Amber Heard. They show old tapes of the couple together all joyous and gushy. In an earlier interview, each claims that they have never been happier and can't imagine life without their partner.

Partner A not only naively believes that UL exists, but also believes that Partner B has conveniently suspended permanently the idea of expectations. But he or she has not. We all have conditions and, unfortunately, they're usually kept secret or not adequately communicated to our lover—or ourselves.

When I hear people come into my office to tell me they will be divorcing, the most common reason I hear is that one of them has changed *after* the wedding. The one who wants out of the relationship claims that they have grown to be almost a different person, and this different person is no longer happy. Some people tell me that this change happens remarkably fast, like a month after they come back from their all-inclusive Sandals honeymoon. And they continue struggling to find an explanation. "Perhaps it was the new child that changed me, or buying the house that was too expensive. All I know is that I've changed. Or maybe she/he's changed."

Here is the rule you have to live by: People don't change. Don't count on people changing. But people's expectations change, or—and this is important—these expectations come to the surface after the marriage.

I Won't Tell You if You Don't Tell Me

The dating couple who merrily go to the movies, have dinner, and then shack up back at their apartment have low expectations, high happiness. But that's only because each of the participants is holding back on revealing what their true expectations are, certainly to the other person, and probably even to themselves.

Let's say the guy doesn't say or express it, but he would like that his future wife be able to bring in a hundred thousand a year from her job. And that she will also be able to bike with him 150 miles per week. But he may not acknowledge any of that during the dating. After all, he thinks to himself, what right do I have to tell her what I expect? We're only dating; we're not married or even engaged.

And by the way, he also loves women with full figures and that's what he is after—tonight. And, if he does tell her that he likes to bike, she will probably respond with something like, "Wow, that sounds like a lot of fun. I love sports, too. I was on the volley ball team in ninth grade."

Let's say that the restaurant was nice, the sex was good, and before you know it, one date leads to twenty, and they now have a relationship—yes, the same guy who initially told himself he wanted a partner to bring in 100K per year, is now with the woman who played volleyball in ninth grade for a few weeks and has that full figure.

Do you see what has happened? The relationship has transformed from a one-night sex romp into a long-term relationship.

In his own mind, he has repressed his expectations and he probably hasn't revealed them to her. Even if she were to ask him directly. "What do you expect of me?" he warmly looks her straight in those big dreamy eyes and answers, "I only expect you to be yourself." And if he is really gushy, he may add, "The only thing I expect of you is that you continue to care about me."

Honey, My Bike Had a Flat—Don't Wait Up for Me

Now, let's skip ahead five years where, surprise-surprise, we find that the couple married a few years before. Now he's complaining to her about the bills. He hasn't had a new car since he got married due to lower family income than expected. "Honey, do you think we are working hard enough to bring in enough money?" he asks. He goes bike riding by himself. Why alone? Because she would rather go do Zumba, or maybe she just had a child and feels inadequately out of shape. Or, she may just not be the athlete she pretended to be when they were dating. Yes, she fooled him. But he fooled himself, too. We do it to each other all the time.

Of course she told herself that she loved him, but she created the expectation mirage of marrying him. So now he is outside biking by himself or with other friends. He may be unhappy because his wife or partner has not met his expectations. Some of the friends that he rides with may be female. And guess what: he eventually meets a lady who also likes to bike ride and they begin to regularly ride together. The UL cycle begins all over again with his new friend. He has no expectations of his new riding friend except the Saturday morning biking. His new friend has no other expectations of him. Do you think they will get along, especially in this low-expectation mode? Of course. He not only has little expectation of her, she satisfies one of his implicit expectations—cycling.

As the weeks pass, he may begin to find reasons to spend more and more time on the bike trail. The poor man then goes home to his wife, head down, and declares to his wife: "I don't know how it happened, but I think I've changed—or maybe we've changed. We are not the same people that we were when we first married. I'm moving out."

In this very simplified illustration, we can see that they really didn't change. She never really did like bike riding, and he never discontinued his expectation that she should accompany him when he cycles. She may have incorrectly created the expectation in his mind she would continue to ride bikes with him after they were married.

If we want to point fingers, then, both parties are to blame. She created the illusion that she would meet an important expectation of his. He betrayed her because he created an expectation mirage about her.

Even as this scenario plays out day after day and marriage after marriage, we still go on thinking romantic love can—and should be—unconditional.

Conditional Love Can be a Game Changer for the Better—If You Bring Your Best Game

Let's say that you are willing to meet me halfway on the proposition that unconditional love, except for parental love or that poor dog locked in the trunk, doesn't really exist for romantic relationships. What does that mean for your day-to-day behavior with your mate?

Initially, your reaction may be one of disappointment and discouragement to think that romantic love lacks a purity if it is not unconditional, that I'm suggesting a cold and mercenary approach and that this book is just another version of Donald Trump's *Art of the Deal*. Does *conditional* love mean, then, that love is just a give and take relationship and a tit for tat, and if I don't get what I expect, I will change my view of you and leave? Absolutely not. Actually, it is just the opposite.

When you come to realize that you cannot operate on the assumption of unconditional love, you will work harder and more optimistically to keep the relationship fresh. You will realize that you cannot assume that everything will just flow and that you can take the relationship for granted. The realization of *conditional* love will encourage you do things you did when the two of you first met and fell in love. It will make you talk with more respect; it will make you understand that even though people may not change, the relationship can. And as hard as it may be to believe, the love could end if you do not do your part to support it.

Even if you have never been married or never had a serious relationship, you probably have witnessed relationships deteriorating because the partners thought that the other person would magically be there forever, regardless of one's behavior or attitude. There was an unconditional agreement to be stuck with each other, which is what we sign up for with a marriage license. Every marriage assumes this bargain. Once you get locked into the relationship, you get locked into the mindset. You've seen what happens. Many times, both partners get lazy with each other and with themselves. They get lazy with telling each other the truth to their partner, especially about expectations. They get lazy about trying to look good for the other spouse and about working hard to continue to deserve their partner's love.

In short, we get lazy about meeting our partner's expectations.

Just because you expect something of your lover doesn't mean you are bad or over-demanding. Realize that we all have expectations. I expect my spouse to be faithful, to be a good parent, to try to look their best, and care for me if I am sick. On the other hand, I love tennis, but my wife never has, so I do not expect her to join me on the tennis court any time soon.

We should not feel guilty about having expectations of our partners. In fact, it is better to understand what our own expectations are as early in the relationship as possible. Conversely, we should not feel indignant or put out that we have to meet expectations of our partner. Therefore, if I have to break away from lounging on the couch in order to accompany my spouse to a baseball game, I will do that because I gladly did it when we dated.

There is another reality that will smack you in the face after you have been in a relationship for a time. Before people have a regular relationship with each other, and when they are just beginning to date, they eat properly, participate in exercise programs, and, yes, read self-help books, as you're doing now. I guarantee you that no one in a happy long-term relationship is reading this. When a person is looking for a relationship, or trying to impress a person in a new relationship, they do not sit around and eat potato chips while watching Jimmy Fallon, or go weeks without washing their underwear. Why? Because they instinctively know that they have to be at their best to catch the love of their life.

And then, with sadness for many, we all know what happens a few years into the relationship. Attitudes tend to change and become more complacent. Almost subconsciously the parties exhibit the behavior which expresses an attitude that says, "Yeah, I've got my mate, we seem to be currently happy with each other, and anyway, she promised me that she would love me for the rest of my life. Hell, she even swore this in front of all our relatives and friends at a church. I'm stuck with her, and let's face it, she's stuck with me—unconditionally." With this inherent attitude, the effort then subsides. The potato chips and ice cream—my favorite—resume as you both now lay on the couch in each other's arms and binge on Netflix.

Mysteriously and magically, the once-fit exercise and self-improvement person is now 25 pounds overweight and takes a bath *after* they've slept with their mate, not before. Ugh.

As I drive down roads in busy suburbs or cities, I make a note of the number of joggers I see. They are mostly young, and these days, often female. I ask myself, why do these young runners risk getting hit by a car and breathe in all that pollution? If we were logical animals, we would see more middle-age overweight people out running, right? The logical person thinks: "I've not had to exercise much through my youth, but now that I've hit 45, I realize that I have a weight problem and exhibit early Diabetes Type 2 symptoms. Oh-oh, I better start exercising and changing my diet. I think I'll jog." But no, I typically do not see that person out running.

How Do I Look in Your Heels, Honey?

A long-standing myth, of course, is that couples have long-term togetherness because of unconditional love. The conventional wisdom of this thought comes out of the question we naturally ask ourselves about any such couple: How else could two people put up with each other so long?

Wrong. Look at two long-term couples we all know.

First, Bruce and Kris Jenner: For a very long period, who had a more successful relationship than that of Kris and Bruce—excuse me—Caitlyn Jenner. They were married 24 years. Both experienced incredible success with reality TV shows, famous children, and tons of money. Eventually, however, Bruce decided that he was done living the lie about his sexual identity. If unconditional love prevails, both partners would have dealt with the situation and toughed it out together.

Aren't we asking too much of Caitlyn to continue leading a false life? Bruce knew that the ultimate *condition* of his ongoing marriage was living life as a man. And even after 24 years of great fame, fortune, and children, Kris understood that these successes could not override the *condition* that Bruce was not allowed to borrow Kris's stiletto heels—or other garments.

Let's talk about another long-term, high-profile marriage—one that survived. George and Barbara Bush were married 73 years, so one would suppose there has to be a helluva lot of UL going on there. Over this long period of togetherness, they experienced just about everything: political ups and downs, the death of a young daughter, trials and tribulations of very active children.

In his eulogy remarks, son Jeb said Barbara described herself as a benevolent dictator. Then he added, "it wasn't always benevolent." Sounds like she had lots of conditions—and this for a homemaker wife who one might think had to be pretty deferential to a president husband and hot-shot kids.

One of my favorite stories about Barbara relates to hubby George getting elected to congress. When most young congressmen go to Washington, they leave their spouse home with the kids so they can work—and perhaps play—in the nation's capital. But Barbara told George, "Forget about moving to DC alone. Get a place big enough for all of us because I'm coming, too, and I'm bringing the kids." She apparently did not depend on unconditional love to maintain a solid marriage, but instead stayed close to her husband physically so they could support each other emotionally. Barbara took nothing for granted.

So, when you hear happy grandparents casually claim they have unconditional love, look a little deeper. They're fooling you, and if *they* really thought about it, they would realize they were fooling themselves, too.

Unconditional Love Sucks!

The Jenners: UL—Almost

J. A. Dougherty

Chapter 3
Can You Pass This Test of a Million Tiny Conditions?

Sam: *"It was a million tiny things that, when you added them all up, meant we were supposed to be together."*
—Movie, *Sleepless in Seattle*, 1993

I know someone who had the most wonderful romance. When he met his future wife, she was a waitress. A newly arrived immigrant, she spoke little English, but she was beautiful and she was sweet. After many visits to the restaurant for take-out, he delivered a single rose to her on Valentine's Day. He asked to take her out for dinner. She may have initially demurred, but the next time agreed, and the date eventually blossomed into a relationship. Several months later they began to share an apartment. In addition to her waitressing, she also attended graduate school for engineering, while he worked a 9 to 5 corporate job. Everything was going well as the relationship moved toward more commitment, marriage plans, and making joint purchases, such as cars and furniture.

I advised them to make sure they understood each other's expectations in the relationship. That is, identify what each of them wanted from their partner and where each would like to be in, say, five years. After they announced plans to marry, I again reminded them about discussing expectations. I mentioned some high-level issues of potential concern, such as the amount of time expected to be spent with each other, which of the two would be the main bread winner, where they would expect to live, indeed, even the country in which each expected to be living. And of course, how many children each desired. And so on.

At the time, the man was also considering a change of careers, transitioning from a somewhat staid corporate position to a more lucrative, but very uncertain, entrepreneurial venture. I asked if they considered the impact on such a move. How would it affect income, time together, location and family stress? If the change in careers leaves him working from home, is she going to like that arrangement? On the other hand, if the new business requires her support, and working with him to get it up and running, is she on board with that? Also, will these factors satisfy *her* expectations of him?

So, you can see that in this case, even when living together there are lots of variables. Partners are participating in various daily activities, coming and going, and having expectations of themselves and the other. Each is asking themselves: What am I going to achieve in my career, how much free time do I want, and with whom do I want to spend my time?

> *When you put expectations of yourself on top of expectations of your lover, you can see what a complicated mess it can be.*

I talked to this couple, and I supplied them with some of my notes. I asked them to complete a questionnaire of what each expected. They were to answer the questions separately and without discussion. Upon completion, they were to exchange answers and honestly evaluate whether compatible expectations existed. They answered the questions independently of each other. They told me, however, that after completion, they didn't discuss the results very much, because *they did not want to upset or surprise the other.*

What?!

But really, isn't that too often what happens? Each person was essentially telling me, "We have our own illusions about the relationship and damn if I am going to break those misconceptions with the truth." To put it another way, they are telling me: "I have my own fantasy about where I want this relationship to go, and if I compare my expectations to those of my partner, they may end up colliding, and there goes the relationship."

Below, I provide duplicate copies of a similar questionnaire, one for you and one for your partner. Feel free to copy or tear the page out when you give written responses. But don't cheat. You're not allowed to review or watch your partner while he or she completes the form. Only when each completes the entire form are you permitted to discuss results.

Warning: Do not answer questionnaire questions trying to anticipate how your partner will answer. That is a formula for misery.

PARTNER QUESTIONNAIRE: MY EXPECTATIONS OF THE RELATIONSHIP

Partner #1 Sheet

Living Arrangement

1. In what location do I want to be living 10 years from now? _____
2. In five years, do I expect to be living in a condo, a small house, medium house, or large house? _____
3. How many hours a week do I expect to work? _____
4. How many hours do I expect my partner to work? _____
5. How many hours per day do I expect to spend with my partner? _____
6. How many times do I like to eat dinner out each week? _____
7. My dream vacation would be: _____
8. I would enjoy having my partner's mother accompany us on vacation. <u>Sure</u>, or <u>not really</u>
9. It will not bother me if future children become identified with my partner's religion. True/False
10. It will not bother me if my partner belongs to a different political party than I. True/False

Finances

11. What do I expect to be earning annually in about ten years? _____
12. What do I expect my partner to be earning in about ten years? _____
13. What do I expect my monthly car payment to be five years from now? $_____
14. How much money do I expect us to save away each year? $_____
15. I expect to have my own checking account separate from my partner's. True/False
16. I expect to get agreement from my partner before I make

Unconditional Love Sucks!

any purchase over $100. True/False
17. I expect my partner to get agreement with me before making any purchase over $100. True/False
18. I expect to keep my pre-marital assets (real estate, car, etc.) titled separately. True/False
19. I expect to keep my pre-marital assets if we get divorced. True/False
20. I expect to have a pre-nuptial agreement if we get married. True/False

Love and Whoopie

21. How many children would I like? _____
22. At what age do I want to be when we start having children? _____
23. Out of a 30-day month, it would be OK if my partner was work-travelling away _____ number of nights.
24. If I see my partner innocently flirting with an attractive person at a party, (circle one) I will or will not be very upset.
25. I expect that I will be hanging out with my friends away from my partner probably about ___ evenings per month.
26. I will be OK if my partner hangs out with his/her friends away from me ____ evenings per month.
27. My partner should probably expect me to get a little drunk or high approximately _____ times per month.
28. I will not have a problem if my partner gets a little drunk approximately _____ times per month.
29. I'm absolutely opposed to using toys during sex. True/False
30. I'm absolutely opposed to our viewing porn during sex. True/False
31. I will be disappointed if my partner were to gain more than _____ pounds.
32. I will be disappointed if my partner spends more than ___ hours per week watching TV or gaming.
33. I will be disappointed if my partner does not spend at least ____ hours per week participating in exercise activities.

PARTNER QUESTIONNAIRE: MY EXPECTATIONS OF THE RELATIONSHIP

Partner #2 Sheet

Living Arrangement

1. In what location do I want to be living ten years from now? _____
2. In five years, do I expect to be living in a condo, a small house, medium house, or large house? _____
3. How many hours a week do I expect to work? _____
4. How many hours do I expect my partner to work? _____
5. How many hours per day do I expect to spend with my partner? _____
6. How many times do I like to eat dinner out each week? _____
7. My dream vacation would be: _____
8. I would enjoy having my partner's mother accompany us on vacation. Sure, or not really
9. It will not bother me if future children become identified with my partner's religion. True/False
10. It will not bother me if my partner belongs to a different political party than I. True/False

Finances

11. What do I expect to be earning annually in about ten years? _____
12. What do I expect my partner to be earning in about ten years? _____
13. What do I expect my monthly car payment to be five years from now? $_____
14. How much money do I expect us to save away each year? $_____
15. I expect to have my own checking account separate from my partner's. True/False
16. I expect to get agreement from my partner before **I** make any purchase over $100. True/False
17. I expect my partner to get agreement with **me** before making any purchase over $100. True/False

18. I expect to keep my <u>pre</u>-marital assets (real estate, car, etc.) titled separately. True/False
19. I expect to keep my pre-marital assets if we get divorced. True/False
20. I expect to have a pre-nuptial agreement if we get married. True/False

Love and Whoopie

21. How many children would I like? _____
22. At what age do I want to be when we start having children? _____
23. Out of a 30-day month, it would be OK if my partner was work-travelling away _____ number of nights.
24. If I see my partner innocently flirting with an attractive person at a party, (circle one) I <u>will</u> or <u>will</u> <u>not</u> be very upset.
25. I expect that I will be hanging out with my friends away from my partner probably about ____ evenings per month.
26. I will be OK if my partner hangs out with his/her friends away from me _____ evenings per month.
27. My partner should probably expect me to get a little drunk or high approximately _____ times per month.
28. I will not have a problem if my partner gets a little drunk approximately _____ times per month.
29. I'm absolutely opposed to using toys during sex. True/False
30. I'm absolutely opposed to our viewing porn during sex. True/False
31. I will be disappointed if my partner were to gain more than _____ pounds.
32. I will be disappointed if my partner spends more than ____ hours per week watching TV or gaming.
33. I will be disappointed if my partner does <u>not</u> spend at least _____ hours per week participating in exercise activities.

How did you do? I hope the results were favorable for the two of you. If you are wondering what happened to my young couple I advised, things did not turn out so well. After telling me they came through the test with flying colors, they married—and divorced two years later. As it turns out, she wanted to move back home to her native country, but he wanted to stay in the U.S. He wanted her to work as an engineer, she wanted to stay home and have children. He needed her help in his new business; she did not want to help him.

Of course they divorced! What did they—and we—expect? Unfortunately, it was not as simple as sitting down together a year later and re-taking the questionnaire, or like reviewing an apartment lease in deciding whether to renew or not. As their *true* expectations and objectives clashed, so did they. The whole thing became an unworkable grind. Internal pressures succumbed to arguments and arguments succumbed to numbing silence and finally terminating drift.

Liar, Liar, Pants on Fire

I see people who go into a relationship under a number of false pretenses to which they fail to admit even to themselves. We may tell ourselves we're madly in love with our new partner, but other underlying reasons are driving our emotions. The list of examples could be a long one. Which of the following false fall-in-love motivations have you been guilty of?

1. Wanting to enter a room with the blond bombshell to impress your friends.
2. Wanting to enter a party with the richest guy in the neighborhood holding your hand.
3. Seeking an additional caregiver for a child.
4. Using a convenient anchor to provide stability while finishing college or medical school.
5. Satisfying the parents' desire for a certain kind of mate, such as religious or ethnic affiliation.
6. Finding a handyman to help maintain a home.
7. Getting revenge against a former lover: "I'll show her by marrying this other woman."
8. Being attracted to the presumed *status* of the other person.

9. Attempting to fix a psychological problem of another that you could not mend for someone in your childhood (e.g., marrying an alcoholic to replace your alcoholic mother).
10. Just finding someone to remove you from a desperate condition (e.g., home, job, or town) in which you believe you currently find yourself.
11. Grabbing the first person who likes you, so you have someone to eat popcorn with at the movies.

Even if you are guilty of some of these false pretense motivations, read the list again *not* as the lover, but as the beloved. Is your new love clinging to you for all the right reasons—or one of the wrong reasons listed above?

In addition to hearing from a divorcing party; "I think I've changed," I also commonly hear, "I think my partner fooled me because he had ulterior motives for marrying me—even though he would never admit it."

If you suspect that your new honeybun fits one of these negative motivations, well, at least you have identified one of their major *expectations* of *you*. You may even look forward to satisfying this expectation. The problem, however—except for the one related to eating popcorn together—none of the items is about sharing companionship. The result could ultimately be a lonely partnership for you.

Expectations can doom a relationship:
1. We don't address our expectations before committing to each other.
2. We have self-illusions about real expectations.
3. One of us—or both—changes expectations later in the relationship.

Even though I don't believe people change, I've seen that as we get older, we may settle down into different activities and perspectives that we did not have at the beginning of a romance. And therefore, as time passes, we can settle into altered expectations.

For instance, assume that a couple mutually shares a desire to be very socially outgoing, including frequent entertaining inside their home. But then, after a long period, one of them finds they desire much less of this lifestyle. They may even begin to resent the attention that their mate receives from others in their circle. They begin to complain, "Why do we always have to be with our friends? Let's just go away ourselves, for a change."

The trials and tribulations of life can wear on us: Job promotions we did not get; miscarriages that tore at our souls; affairs we had to forgive; getting jilted by the love of our life; parents dying; putting on that extra 40 pounds. All eventually chip away at our fresh college can-do spirit. Such changes are difficult to predict. I get depressed just listing them.

At a point later in our lives, expectations truly may change. Prepare yourself and your partner to address inevitable change with directness, flexibility, and communication. And don't forget some good professional counselling, too.

The questionnaire in this chapter is just the start in evaluating potential relationship success. Underlying attitudes, ingrained personality styles, and mental health issues are all lurking around the corner—and in the following chapters.

Part Two

CREATING THE RIGHT CONDITIONS FOR LOVE SUCCESS

So far, we've talked about how often the best kind of love is conditional love, in which each partner tries to continually bring their best to the relationship to keep it satisfying and alive.

But, even with all this, the experienced financial counselor in me wants to tell you about additional facets you'll have to manage and evaluate in your perspective mate if you want to have happy days ahead—instead of just a lot of crappy nights.

J. A. Dougherty

Chapter 4
Forget Gypsy Psychics—Your Lover's Parents Predict the Future

John Beckwith: *"Rule 16: Give me an up-to-date family tree."*
—Movie, *The Wedding Crashers*, 2005

Norman Bates: *"A boy's best friend is his mother."*
—Movie, *Psycho,* 1960

When we get into a relationship, we all want to peer into the crystal ball and ask ourselves, what will this person I'm with really be like after I get to know them? How will they behave a year from now or five years after I marry him? What we are really asking: How will they be after I'm stuck with them?

The answer is closer than we think. More times than not, you just have to look at Mom and Dad—theirs, not yours. People tell us we are what we eat, but that's only half the story. We really are who our parents are. When all is said and done, it's hard to win the war against family traits. The reason mother-in-law jokes are so timeless is that men fall in love with the daughter, but end up married to her mother. Before we get married, we love the daughter and put up with the mother-in-law.

Fathers-in-law are not immune either. . . How many times have we heard, "He drinks too much like his old man. . . Why didn't I see it before I married him? . . . He's a chip off the old block. "

We could fill another book with the many clichés about in-laws.

Sir, What is Your Pedigree?

I have lived in a traditional southern county for many years and was at a luncheon one day when an elderly gentleman with deep roots in the community, and the father of a U.S. congressman, approached me. Upon hearing my name, he asked, without irony or humor, "Sir, what is your pedigree?" In one breath I was offended that he wanted to classify me, but at the same time flattered with a guilty self-approval that he was willing to accept me into his realm if I had a satisfactory response. But his question got right to the point. He believed that if he could connect me to a family with which he was familiar, he would automatically have knowledge of my traits, my upbringing, and probably what to expect of me. His ingrained view: You are how you're bred; you are what your parents are.

Nurtured by Nature, or Natured by Nurture?

We've all heard the old debate about whether someone is influenced by their environment or their genes. Is it nature or nurture? It doesn't matter for us in this discussion. Statistics simply show that if someone's parents are psychopaths, their kids are more likely to be psychopaths. Whether it was because of some genes passed down or just because everybody in the clan liked to sit around and beat each other up, there is going to be a higher likelihood that junior will want to do that, too. The result is the same. There is a higher chance we will be dealing with a person who has a problem, or suffers some other personality disorder.

It's amazing that when we see the parents who have behavioral problems related to things such as drugs or constant job changes, and we observe those same traits in their child—our lover—we conveniently make excuses for the person. We tell ourselves, "Oh, my Bob just likes to have fun", or "He's going through a stage. He's really a good guy. I know his father has problems, but I'm not worried, because I know his son—my boyfriend—will be different."

Don't bet your life on it.

Maybe the girlfriend of Stephen Paddock, the gunman who killed dozens of people at a Las Vegas concert a few years ago, should have asked about *his* father. She would have found out that Dad was a convicted bank robber and described by the FBI as psychopathic with suicidal tendencies. Now that's some pedigree.

Unconditional Love Sucks!

You have to keep your eyes open. The best way to do this is to watch how the parents function. If the parents are a little nuts, most likely the kids will be a little nuts, too. And maybe a lot nuts.

 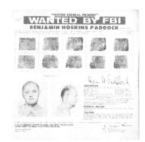

Stephen Paddock and dear old dad Benjamin Paddock: Has your lover's father been wanted by the FBI?

Evaluating Parents

I've talked about assessing the parents to determine what your mate will be like in the future. And, of course, it's easy if the father is a convicted bank robber, the mother is a drug dealer, and your boyfriend or girlfriend has a record for shoplifting. But, unfortunately, it's usually not that black and white. More typically, the mother may drink too much at parties, and the father lives in another state and has changed jobs frequently, but is generally a nice guy.

And then there are siblings. There's the brother about whom people comment: "He's adjusted so well to a difficult family environment. He's overcome the challenges, and he's turned out nice, anyway." If you find yourself using this same language to describe your new heartthrob to your friends and family, watch out. You may realize only too late that he or she may not have overcome *all* of the challenges.

In High School, He Wasn't a Bank Robber

While our partner is growing up, many of their problems are camouflaged behind a structured life that prevents others—and ourselves—from understanding them clearly. When in school, they follow a curriculum of class schedules and tests and pre-ordained holidays. Even in college, they have semesters to follow, papers to write, and homecoming games to attend. Their structured life during this period takes much of the decision-process away, and as a result, it is difficult to assess our partner's ability to make good decisions, because they may not be making many life decisions to begin with.

During this structure-imposed time, the inner voices that drive people may not be evident. For instance, have you attended your high school reunion, only to be surprised to hear that the star quarterback on the football team became the town drug dealer? God, what a pity about Timmy, we say to each other. What was in him—what voices did he hear—that drove him to that life? Conversely, we meet the guy at the reunion who achieved just average grades and had pimples, but now owns six BMW dealerships and is married to Miss Gorgeous. How did Sam pull that off, we wonder? In high school, we didn't know he had it in him.

Given the locked-in structure of school, many people manage to get by pretty well. It's only when they leave and go out into the world, where many decisions await, do they perhaps falter—and falter big. Their inner voices take over in the vacuum. Many argue whether it's environment, hormones, or genes. Well, somebody else's book can figure that out. We just know that as people move to unstructured adulthood, they can start to do weird—and often destructive—things.

A favorite pastime these days is talking about the historically high rate of millennials still home, living with parents. I know that the conventional explanation revolves around high student debt and the inability to find a good job, but let's look at another level of this phenomenon. When the adult child leaves the structured world of education and then must decide what they are going to do, it appears many have difficulty with this. In the past, it has not been typical for a young adult, in the prime of their child-bearing years, to be still home under the shelter of their parents. We may ask ourselves: What voices are *these* young people hearing? Are they afraid? Are they lazy? Are they too immature to make a decision about what to do in life? Are they perhaps afraid of disappointing their parents?

Whatever the answer, you may not really know how the person

is going to behave in the unstructured world of adulthood until he or she confronts that world—or at least until they move out of mom's basement.

When people are seeking financial and marital advice from me, and they tell me that their partner's entire family is wacko, except for their lover, they sometimes ask me about marriage strategies. I usually tell them to slow down and just be together for some number of years. If the two of you love each other, why can't you wait, say, five years, especially if you think you are going to go through all of life together? Decide to personally commit to your relationship, but don't bind yourselves financially or legally, and certainly don't have children. Just enjoy each other.

If, after five years, no psychosis (a loss of touch with reality) appears, or the triple AAA hasn't occurred (i.e. abuse, addiction, adultery), then things will probably fall into place.

Bottom line for Youth Dating: In high school and often in college, we really don't know who the real person is. The next best thing: Take a look at their parents.

A note to parents of dating children: I strongly believe that your child needs guidance when choosing their mate. If you think your son or daughter is dating a bum or a loser, diplomatically tell them so. You can't dwell on it or be overly emotional when communicating your feelings. Perhaps do it in terms of questions, such as, "Why do you think Betty dropped out of high school?" or, "Do you think Joe drinks too much?" or, "Why does Mary have 55 tattoos on her body?" Make them aware of people you have known who are like their partners who have had lots of problems in life. Or hand them a copy of this book. Good luck in getting them to read it.

At Least She's Not Fat Like Her Mother

In chapter five, we're going to talk about how a person's physical beauty really is only skin deep. But if that's still very important to you, and you want to see what your partner is going to resemble—physically and mentally—25 years from now, look at their parents. So, if you don't like wooly men, but his father looks like a grizzly bear with pants, watch out. If you don't like portly ladies, and her mother weighs 300 pounds, perhaps plan for a stronger bed. If you are overly preoccupied by these likelihoods, the only consolation I can offer is that by the time *you* are fifty, you will probably be fat and hairy, too.

Ah, I know what you're thinking: "His or her mother and father might be ____blank____ (pick a bad trait) but my boyfriend is so different." Yeah, but that's what he is like *now*, when he is a youthful 25 and trying his best to make a good impression. Similarly, do you know many people who pick their nose—or their butt—during a first date? I don't either

Meet My Granddaddy Who Fought in the Civil War

Another way to tell if your partner is of good pedigree is to check their life expectancy. It sounds screwy, but long life is a sign of not only good physical genes, but good mental stability. In my years of practice, virtually every client who lives to reach their 90s not only has adequate physical abilities, they absolutely excel in their mental health. They have a good outlook, do not suffer depression, have a fun sense of humor, are nice to others, and are optimistic. In my informal survey of old-age survivors, mental health is even more important than physical health.

I have observed that mean people die earlier than nice people. I have seen it over and over. However, I have also seen the hostile person, through their stressful behavior, wear out their nicer partner to the point where their partner dies—I think just to escape the mean rat!

For the record, I have very few, if any, clients who live into their 90s that smoke, drink a lot, or who do not eat normally. Interestingly, my long-lifers are normally *not* health nuts. I remember recently sitting at a restaurant with a lady who was 101. While the rest of us labored over the menu to find the grilled fish and heathiest salad, she ordered fried chicken and French fries, and she reminded the waiter not to forget her a dish of vanilla ice cream with chocolate syrup for dessert. Are you ready for this: Vegetarians statistically do not live as long as carnivores. Why? Experts are not sure, but they think it is related more to the person's mental rather than physical health. A female acquaintance who has regularly internet dated in the New York City area recently told me that she would love to meet a modern man who simply ate like a normal human being. Instead, too many of them over-study the menu, tediously cross-examine the waiter, and when the special-order meal finally arrives at the table, they'll stare at it, pick through it with a fork, then carefully nibble, as if the food has been poisoned by a clandestine busboy.

When you think about celebrities who die before old age, it's not because of cancer or falling off a mountain, instead it's usually related to poor mental health. Michael Jackson, Amy Winehouse, Whitney Houston and of course Elvis compose a small list of such examples. None of them had stable love lives either.

What's My Darling Daughter Doing with a Bum Like You?

We can't finish talking about parents unless we mention the other extreme. Sizing up your partner's parents can also go the other way. If his parents are over-achievers, have nothing whatsoever out of place in their home, and they expect their son to be a Harvard PhD by the time he's old enough to drive, much of their vigor may pass down to your dreamboat. You can probably expect a very demanding mate. If you enjoy lounging on the couch in your dirty underwear, with buttered popcorn dribbling out of your mouth while binge-watching reality shows, forget it. You may want to stay away from this family. You will be glad to learn, however, that if you are this kind of slouch, the family will probably reject *you* before you get a chance to give *them* the snub. When you walk through the door, they're immediately inspecting the merchandise. Remember that pedigree stuff I told you about.

And do not naively fool yourself into believing the parents like you if they are superficially polite to you. Of course they are going to be nice to you. You're the new package of meat in the room accompanying their precious child.

Dad, Meet my New Main Squeeze

As parents of young people who are dating now, my wife and I find ourselves asking our children these questions first: Oh, how nice that you have found someone, but by the way, what are her parents like? What do her parents do? Are they still married?

It's almost instinctive among parents to ask these types of questions. But it amazes me when kids respond with, "I don't know, I didn't ask, and I haven't met the parents. Actually, I don't even know if they're still alive. "

I think, with age, we've intuitively learned the lesson of a person's pedigree. The sooner *you* learn it, the better off you'll be.

Doctors use family history to predict illness and disease, such as cancer, heart problems, and diabetes. Shouldn't we do the same thing to learn about inherited personality traits?

Two of the most important things you want to see in parents are honesty and integrity. Do they cheat on their income taxes? Do you catch the parent making little white lies to their children or friends? Honesty and integrity are so critical, but they are one of those things that are hard to change and hard to fake. You either have it or you don't. If you also come up short in this area, don't worry, the bad Karma will catch up to you, too.

I found during my long years in practice that the world of people can be divided into two halves. One half is basically honest and works hard and tries to do the right thing. The other half thinks they are smarter than the average Joe, believes they can cheat their spouse, the IRS, their boss, and always be one step ahead of everyone else. And that's how they live their lives, unscrupulously struggling to stay just one step ahead.

It's like the late Bernie Madoff, who died in jail because he defrauded thousands with a devious Ponzi financial scheme. In its simplest definition, a Ponzi scheme is one in which the money manager takes money from one client and uses it to create artificial income for another client, and then continues this cycle as more clients come aboard. The schemer hopes that new clients keep coming in to pay the old ones back. Yes, they always believe they can fool everyone—and stay one step ahead of them. It never ends happily, but as I write this, an investment manager somewhere is probably doing a Ponzi scheme and thinking he can outsmart the system. I just hope that you are not sleeping with him or enjoying his boat.

I have followed this type of person for years and have watched the debris they leave in their trail. They'll go through a bankruptcy, get fired several times, owe the IRS money, get arrested for a bar fight, or be in trouble for late child support payments. Don't be part of the debris.

You may be sleeping with the child, but you end up marrying the parents.

You should step back and analytically ask yourself, what *are* his parents really like? What are *her* parents like?

Parents? What Parents?

Of course, when your boyfriend or girlfriend hesitates to introduce you to their parents, raise the red flag. It's worth repeating: If your new love casually says that he or she has an uncomfortable or non-existent relationship with their parents, look out. I've heard these lines more than once: "I haven't spoken to my parents in five years, but we have an understanding." Or: "I really don't get along with my father." What? If they don't get along with one of the two people nature meant them to always get along with, something is wrong. If they can't get along with someone who has probably spent most of their life feeding them, cleaning their poop, and forgiving them, then, Houston, we have a problem.

I know what you're saying: "Why should I blame my lover for his parents' faults. It's not that *he's* the jerk. He doesn't talk to them because *they* are the jerks." But remember that we are not talking about blame. We are attempting to discover issues and traits that your partner will bring to you. We do not hold it against your parents for giving you a tendency for high cholesterol—not vindictively, anyway—but this is a trait you have inherited.

All right, let's pretend that your lover is a wonderful person, but she was abused by one or both parents. For those of us who have not been abused, it may be impossible to realize the impact of being hurt, minimized, and ridiculed, or worse, just unloved, by a parent. It's a tough break to endure. Some children come out OK and understand what they have gone through and can perhaps recover. But most children have difficulty recovering. They frequently use their new lover as therapy. As a result, you are not only their shrink, you assume the role of substitute parent as well. Ugh.

In addition to passing down genetic traits and environmental behavior, parents also pass down family traditions. Religious traditions, political traditions, and even how they eat a dinner. By watching the parents' traditions, you will learn what your partner's traditions will be.

If you like her family's traditions, that's wonderful, because you will be living them, if not tomorrow, then someday.

Do you want proof of inherited traditions? Notice that many children of Republicans are also Republicans. Same for children of Democrats. Moreover, children often follow the same religion as their parents. If we sit back and think about this behavior objectively, it makes little sense. Here we have a young person going out into the world, meeting many people from different walks of life, even perhaps going to college and taking various critical thinking classes (I hope!). There are dozens of religions from which to choose. But how many children of Baptists become Buddhists? Not many. Your lover may have given more thought and deliberation to which color he'll paint the bathroom than to his religious affiliation. But you'll have a greater chance of convincing him to paint his walls in pink polka dots than persuading him to change his church.

My Father was Charles Manson, But I'm Different

Let's put some flesh and bone on this parent thing and come up with some real people you know about. How would you feel about your child dating the child of sex goddess Marilyn Monroe? Actually, she had no children, which was probably fortunate. I know it would be fun for the notoriety and for the bragging rights to date her kid, and Marilyn's child would probably be pretty good looking. But think of the multi-layered issues her child would bring to a relationship, given such an environment and gene pool.

OK, easy enough. But what do you think about dating the

daughter of actors Alec Baldwin and Kim Basinger? That may be a difficult call for our male readers who have seen recent pictures of daughter Ireland Baldwin. Here's another tricky one: dating the daughter of Bill and Hillary Clinton. We have two very intelligent and driven parents, on the one hand. But we know that Hillary is known for some very mean streaks, while Bill is known on the other hand, for . . . well, we know what Bill is known for. Even if daughter Chelsea is well adjusted, as she certainly appears to be, as her mate, you should expect an environment of constant high demands, achievement, and challenging expectations.

As you can see, we are not just focusing on typical losers like druggies and deadbeats who can make your life miserable. We're talking about all the characteristics that come with parents and which are probably passed down to the children.

Be very frightened if you hear yourself saying: "I know his parents are Charles Manson types, but he is not like them; he's different."

Elvis, It's a Pleasure Dating Your Daughter

For the fun of it, and for you to practice becoming aware of the family traits your partner will inherit, review the chart below. It identifies various celebs and some of their salient traditions. Given the information provided, would you want to date their son or daughter? Or go as far as walking down the aisle with them?

J. A. Dougherty

Celebrity Couple	Family Tradition/ Focus	Would you date their child?	Would you marry their child?
Donald/Melania	Bombast/Money/Beauty		
Bill/Hillary	Politics/Money/Resolve		
Jenner/Kardashian	Ambition/Publicity		
Elvis/Priscilla	Music/Divorce/Drugs		
George/Laura Bush	Ambition/Southern Religion/Politics		
Taylor Swift	Work/Work/Work		
Lindsay Lohan/Anyone	Chaos/Chaos/Chaos		
Johnny/Amber	You fill in the blank		

Lisa Marie Presley: Died young—like dad

 It's difficult to summarize a collection of family traditions and traits in a chart, but you get the idea. The Kardashians and Bushes, in one respect, have many things in common—like money, fame, and hard work. But, if you are dating one of their children, we both know that you are walking into entirely different traditions.

 And speaking of hard work, the capacity for working hard and the pursuit of excellence is a characteristic most on the chart share—yes, especially the Kardashians, believe it or not—or else

Unconditional Love Sucks!

we would not be aware of these people in the first place. All couples listed have shown a life-sacrificing devotion to their goals. That, in itself, will probably be an important tradition passed down to their children.

Complete the chart for your partner's family, too. Don't be afraid to expand the list of major family traditions beyond my typical three.

Toil and Trouble?

Now that you're an expert in evaluating family traits, consider this case study of a mystery couple and tell me—figuratively, of course—what you think their chances are of long- term success.

First, the groom. His parents were divorced early on, and one of them was tragically killed accompanying a new boyfriend. Not only were the groom's own parents divorced, three of four of his father's siblings were also divorced. On top of all this, the groom's job prospects are very cloudy.

Next, the bride. She is not on speaking terms with her half-brother and sister, both of whom she grew up with. Indeed, she had trouble finding a family member or close friend to walk her down the aisle, including her own father who did not even attend the wedding. If that's not enough, she gave up a pretty good job to move to her husband's hometown.

How much would you bet on this marriage? If you believe these two are headed for challenges, you're too late to do anything about it. Prince Harry has already married Meghan Markle—with about two billion witnesses looking on.

When I expressed my observations about the couple to some friends, I was rebuffed along the lines I described earlier. They admonished me, "Oh, Harry and Meghan are great; their family is just crazy. Don't blame them." You see, we just have so much difficulty evaluating the petri dish because we desire so very much a happily-ever-after life, no matter if it's with Harry the Prince or Herman the plumber.

Mom, You Don't *Need* to Know His Name—He was a Speed Date

In the celebrity chart above, there is included both a dating and marrying column, because my friends tell me all the time that they could date so-and-so, but would certainly stop short of marriage. However, I have seen few such lines drawn in the sand. More often than one might initially believe, a dinner date leads to a one-night stand—or vice versa—which leads to more dating, which leads to an implied commitment, and before you know it, you're buying real estate in joint names with the Boston Strangler.

I know this advice is contrary to the speed-dating philosophy found on such popular sites as Tinder, which provides fast and noncommittal hook-ups for—let's face it—one-night stands. The people I know on Tinder swear that they do not care about long-term relationships and that the other partner knows this, too.

Bull!

Another person who uses Tinder was more honest with me. He tells me that he is indeed using the service to find his marriage partner, and the internet dating concept gives him a platform to easily hunt and move on, and then hunt and move on some more. Sometimes it's fun, sometimes it's not. Ironically, when he thought that he found Miss Right, she didn't think he was Mr. Right, so she did what he typically does: Move on to the next speed date, leaving him stuck with the Uber fare.

Too frequently, once you get sucked into a relationship, it is difficult to get—for a lack of a better term—sucked out of it.

Let Ann Figure It Out

You have to almost split your personality to objectively evaluate your partner. I know a professional golfer—we'll call her Ann—and I have asked her how she manages to control her nerves when she makes that critical putt while thousands and even millions watch. How do you get that relaxed stroke when you know there is so much depending on this one shot? Weekend golfers know this phenomenon of nerves all too well: It feels so easy to take those nice, relaxed practice swings. Then two seconds later, when it counts, you stand over the ball and what happens? Every nerve in your body seems to freeze and become nonfunctional. I think the same thing happens when we're in love. Many of our analytical brain waves go haywire.

Well, what Ann told me surprised and almost stunned me. Before the shot, she completely *splits* her mind into two personalities. In addition to her Ann personality, who analyzes the shot and the distance and the wind, she creates another person in her mind, whom she has named Bobbie. Bobbie, her imagined companion, is carefree and only out to have a fun time. Bobbie is the one who makes the nice relaxed swing, because she doesn't give a shit who's watching!

In our everyday life, we don't permit our Ann to evaluate our partner or his parents because we are afraid of the potential findings. If we think there may be problems, we brush them aside and revert to what we think we have to depend on for a back-up, catch-all, problem-solver that will allow everything to work out: Unconditional Love.

As you fall in love, let your Bobbie have the fun, but let your Ann evaluate the parents—and everything else.

Chapter 5
Falling for Successful and Beautiful People—the Ugly Realities

"Oh, no. It wasn't the airplanes. It was beauty that killed the beast."
—Movie, *King Kong*, 1933

One of the great ironies of life is that we always pursue beauty and success in our romantic endeavors, but they often bring along disaster. Just ask Kong.

Why on earth is a financial advisor writing a chapter about beauty? What does that stuff have to do with money?

Everything.

Money, like beauty, draws other people in, often with more force than a tornado devouring everything in its path.

We can never forget that as biological beings, we are pursuing the Darwinian plan of looking for people who are better than ourselves and who are more beautiful.

Darwin was a scientist who famously figured out evolution and natural selection. He termed the selective mating process "sexual selection". Like it or not, humans are in this game, too.

That means we instinctively pursue the good-looking girl, the handsome guy and the good income earner. And these days, the guy may be pursuing the female who is the good income earner. This pursuit allows the human race to improve generation after generation. It's probably why we can run faster and are taller than our grandparents.

The pursuit of someone who has superior qualities is only negative when we fail to see the whole picture. In this chapter, let's take a look at some of the pitfalls that may accompany a narrow view of chasing Darwin's theory.

So now I guess you're thinking that, gee, does that leave me to marry somebody who is uglier than I am or dumber than I am, or picks their nose more than I do? Well, that's the secret to this messy process. You need to find somebody in your range of qualities, sort of like the aphorism that says there is a soulmate for every soul. I think that's true.

Another aphorism says that most of us love sausage, but we don't want to see how it is made. Romance is the same say. We all dream about walking down the aisle and living happily ever after, but the ups and downs, wrong turns, and pain in eventually even *getting* to the aisle is indeed messy—for some of us, probably even worse than if we had to make sausage.

At the Risk of Stereotyping

In addition to focusing on physical beauty or intelligence, another area where we commonly see the sexual selection process, at least in the past, is the person being attracted to the successful business-lawyer-doctor type. The reason is obvious: We drive down the street of the affluent neighborhoods with the beautiful homes and manicured lawns and think that life must be so sweet for these people. "Please, God, if I could only catch someone who could give me that kind of life style—the kind I truly deserve." We all want to be married to the successful person so we can live on Sweet Street, too.

Here's the good news for those envious under-achievers among us: that which I see happen is often not so sweet. Remember that if you marry a very successful person, they normally had to work really hard to get there and they're probably an over-achiever in many respects. That ambition may be hard to keep up with. Expect that other people will be attracted to them just as you were. Be prepared for some kick-ass romance competition, even after the wedding bells ring.

Is it any mystery that Donald Trump is able to marry beautiful and smart women? Remember what each party is getting here. The beautiful woman is getting a superior income generator and upper status profile. Mr. Trump is getting a superior beauty with lots of intelligence. You don't think Melania's bright? Do you really think an over-achiever like the Trumpster would accept a partner who isn't?

Unconditional Love Sucks!

A bed of roses for Melania?

Such a high-powered relationship is not all a bed of roses. Just ask Mrs. Trump. For someone like Trump to be successful, he's had to work hard, be very demanding of themselves and others, and probably have a pretty healthy ego. It's just not as simple as marrying a successful person who works during the day, comes home at night, pets the dog, and kisses his partner, passively moving through life. Most financially successful people I know move through life like a bulldozer, shoveling some people up, pushing others aside, and dragging the rest along. He or she is probably working late, never home, perhaps flirting with other people in the office, and demanding that you drop everything so you can drive to a party with his friends this weekend. And when he or she arrives home, they ignore the dog, become demanding, and show little interest in what you might have done with your life today. Then after dinner, they are on their cell phone communicating with colleagues. The need to achieve never stops.

And it's not just the likes of Donald Trump. Could you to be married to a Justin Bieber or Taylor Swift? Obviously, Trump, Bieber, and Swift are very different people, but each would be very demanding of a partner. Talk about making sausage!

And, the more successful they are, the more inclined they are to spread their seed of immortality to other people. Consciously or not, over-achievers truly believe that they are God's Gift to the World. As a result, they are often driven to spread their genes—and fluids—to other partners. Who knows what voices someone like Bill Clinton and Donald Trump hear. But one of these quiet inner voices may whisper; "Hey, I am entitled to do this because I am so smart, powerful, and good looking that I need to spread my genes among humanity." I suppose one could say that this is the biological view. There is also the egotistical view: I am entitled to do this promiscuous activity because I'm so damn wonderful—and I can get away with it.

We keep picking on Trump and Clinton, but we can certainly add all of the other infamous characters caught up in the MeToo movement, including Harvey Weinstein, Charlie Rose, and Matt Lauer. It sure sounds like they had an attitude of entitlement. And yes, this list of names is clearly overweighted with men.

When you link up to an over-achiever, or worse, a good-looking over-achiever, be prepared for many of these factors. We see it all the time. We can never figure out why someone like a Bill Clinton or Bill Cosby would risk so much to experience the fling on the side. Yes, they got caught. And yes, at this writing, Cosby is still married to the same wife—for almost 60 years.

I do not have many famous celebrities as clients, but I have had several successful business and physician clients. And all day long, their ego is being fed by others who work for them or depend on them, including the pretty woman or the sexy guy. "Thank you for the raise and the promotion, Mr. Smith." "Thanks for getting me the great legal settlement, Ms. Baker." "You saved my husband's life, Dr. Jones." Can you understand, now, why achievers would harbor a feeling of entitlement, and even thrill, for making their own rules?

Most over-achievers are raised to be driven and succeed, and they may have some deep desire to overcome and prove something.

Honey, You are So Beautiful—When the Room is Really Dark

So, what do you do if you think you don't want to chase somebody who is a male model with no brains, but you don't want the ugliest person in the room either? Try looking for a beautiful aspect of that person you feel comfortable with who compiles a good mix of overall qualities.

There's an old saying: "When you turn the lights off in the bedroom, your homely lover looks as beautiful as Mr. or Miss America." If you forget that, you may eventually live to regret it. One morning you could awake, instead, to have breakfast with someone who's a good-looking jerk.

It's sometimes surprising that with our supposed sophistication, when we meet people, we still instinctively judge them more on looks than personality. As a result, we are more accepting of greatly flawed behavior than of unsatisfactory appearance. It gets back to the myth of believing that we can change their behavior if it sucks, but not their appearance, which we think we're stuck with.

But, do not lose hope if your lover is no Beyoncé. You *may* be able to change that. Do an exercise and diet program together. Help with clothes and hairstyling. Yes, I realize there are limits. Then you just dim the lights and take out your contact lenses and enjoy each other.

If they're an extreme physical wreck, though, be careful. If they have not washed their hair for three weeks or they weigh 500 pounds, they may have serious problems beyond your first-aid skills. Unless you really like washing hair. Or you weigh 500 pounds, too.

The one thing you also want to avoid is to unnecessarily limit your options with the "type" that you believe you like. Example: Say that I especially like tall blondes, and are, therefore, the only ones I hope to date. Or, I have tattoos, so unless his body is also 80% printed, he doesn't get to meet my parents. By doing that, you preclude yourself from being with all those other wonderful people who are not tall blondes or have multiple tattoos exhibiting each phase of their life.

Send for the Maid, I'm Feeling Romantic

Do you ever wonder why really good-looking couples have affairs with other partners? We ask ourselves: Wow, their spouse is so beautiful, how could he or she cheat? The list among celebrities in this category goes on forever. Christie Brinkley, one of the most famous supermodels of all time, had a husband who played around with the nanny—someone obviously not as beautiful as his Christie. Or Arnold Schwarzenegger having the affair—and child—with a domestic worker who was clearly no Sofia Vergara. He could have theoretically had anyone, but he ended up with the homely housemaid. Notice that each of these affairs were with people who were very close by, very handy. The perpetrator almost seems to be shouting out that, "I'm just not getting enough satisfaction from my own spouse; I don't really care whom I have sex with."

If you marry somebody for beauty, don't forget that physical beauty usually declines over time—unless you're with Jenifer Lopez, of course. So, if you are thinking of getting a trophy wife or husband, she/he may not look beautiful 25 years from now. If this happens, will there be any magic left for you? Apply this test: Pretend that your beautiful lover has a car accident tomorrow and is terribly scarred and disfigured. Would you still want have dinner with them—say, over the next ten years??? Yes, I'll let you assume it's a dark, very dark, restaurant.

And that's not the worst of it. As years go on, the beautiful person in the relationship also knows their beauty is vanishing. Is that going to make them more insecure? Usually it does. How do you think they respond to this? And it doesn't matter whether they are the lifeguard at the community pool or a movie star. They often feel justified in taking actions that hurt the relationship, including a mid-life crisis, substance abuse, and affairs.

Am I Gorgeous? Gee, I Didn't Notice

Don't believe the line when you hear someone say, "Oh, I don't see myself as attractive," or "I don't think of myself as good looking." Virtually everyone who is attractive knows it. They not only know they're beautiful, they usually know how to use it to their advantage. How do they know to do this? It is instinctive and reactive. Studies point out that pretty faces and hunks get more attention from others, more deference from those they deal with, and yes, better tables at a restaurant. This power certainly also extends to the work place to get a job, close a sale, or obtain a promotion. Beautiful people become accustomed to this special treatment.

A word to those of my readers who are beautiful, both male and female. Yes, you know who you are, too. I'm aware that you may take what advice I lay out here for the less-beautiful and use it to your advantage. Many things in life may change with technology and sexual norms, but not this aspect of life. To the Kim Kardashians and Brad Pitts of the world, I say go for it; utilize your beauty to get ahead and live an enriched life. But be careful not to abuse your power, because I can also predict bad karma coming back to bite you in your cute derrière.

There are studies of people's reactions to beautiful people. Researchers have set up situations in which an ugly man approaches a woman and gives her an offbeat comment. Her reaction is understandably cold and aloof with a general reaction of "Why did you say such a weird thing to me?" Next, researchers had a good-looking, well-dressed guy approach the same woman a bit later and say virtually the same thing in the same way. You can guess her reaction: She found the comment amusing and entertaining, and she was much more engaged.

The study, of course, refutes the need for coming up with the so-called clever "pick-up" line. If you're good looking, don't worry about what you say, but on the other hand, if you're a dog, you may struggle even if reciting Shakespeare.

The presence of beauty is an overwhelming power that controls us. Therefore, if you are at the receiving end of it (that is, the other person is the more beautiful), be aware of it and try to control your own reactions to it. Also, do not stop analyzing other factors that reveal the real person, as we discuss throughout this guide.

Do Not Marry Your Stripper—Probably

Despite the experiment with pick-up lines, women tend to react somewhat differently than men to the physical beauty of their sexual partner. The best way to illustrate this difference is to visit two different erotic dance clubs: one, the typical gentleman's bar, and the other, any place where women go to see male Chippendale dancers. As difficult as it may be, for our discussion here, don't look at the dancers. Instead, observe each of the respective audiences. When men watch live porn, they are usually very focused, mesmerized, and lost in serious contemplation. You might think there was a life-and-death event happening. On the other hand, what do females do when faced with a gyrating male torso? Giggle, laugh, and joke with their girlfriends.

Why the difference? I can only guess on this one, but I believe the female system is a little better at putting beauty of the opposite sex in proper perspective. The female intuitively knows that, although a factor, appearance is not the only element in partner selection and probably should not be the deciding one.

Notwithstanding the more well-rounded perspective of females, I would like to think that my book—or any book—can help level the playing field between the beautiful and not-so-beautiful, but it never will. The starting point for the handsome will always be ahead of those who are not.

I'm Pretty, So I Must be a Nice Person

When you watch the stars on television and in the movies, everybody is beautiful, and they appear oh-so friendly and disarming. Therefore, we want to believe all beautiful people must be really nice. Don't forget that most people in the movies *have* to be beautiful—because we probably would not sit there and watch the same old action plot if they weren't. Hollywood knows this, too.

Often the pretty people in movies, especially romantic comedies, are not only sweet, their characters often portray a person who is vulnerable, innocent, and even confused. For many beautiful people in real life, it is more typically just the opposite. Their beauty gives them the confidence to go out and get what they want, achieve, and climb that Darwinian sexual selection path. I state this with no malice or resentment.

In the movie, *The Devil Wears Prada*, do you really think that if Anne Hathaway's character really looked like Anne Hathaway, with those full pouty lips and brown eyes bigger than coffee mugs, she would have gotten—or put up with—the crap she did on her first day on the job? No way. I don't care what rags she may have worn. In real life, even her bitchy boss, played by Meryl Streep, would have been a lot nicer to someone of Hathaway's beauty.

Who has more charisma, money, and looks than Charlie Sheen? His mom and dad would probably even pass the parent survey in chapter four. How did he turn out so nuts? But even so, would you have fallen for him? I probably would have, too.

While we are talking about beautiful movie stars, can you think of any who have had long term marriages? I can't either. Older readers may remember an exception: Paul Newman and Joanne Woodward—both big stars and beautiful people—were married 50 years. A word more about the Newmans in the last chapter.

Exclude Beauty and Wealth as Conditions to Love?

If we could exclude beauty and wealth as conditions, perhaps our divorce rate would be much lower, but we probably couldn't run as fast.

But nor can we imagine a dating website that excludes photos or a person's profession. If unconditional love existed, it shouldn't matter if I'm fat or skinny, a plumber, or a surgeon. You just need to know that I like dogs, my favorite movie is *Mission Impossible 7* and I love Chinese food.

The bottom line: Try to count the Chinese food as much as the fact that he or she is a surgeon. It may make for many more pleasant meals.

Money and beauty bring conditions to a relationship like nothing else.

Chapter 6
Every Action Gets a Reaction—in Love, Too

"Some old wounds never truly heal, and bleed again at the slightest word."
—TV Show, *Game of Thrones*, George R.R. Martin

Unfortunately, too many of us live by another quote from the same drama: "When you play a game of thrones, you win or die." In romance, however, this proposition is not true. It is a myth, just like unconditional love. In a successful relationship, you don't win, you give—and that's good, not bad.

To begin with, if you understand this next sentence fully, there's no reason to even read the rest of the chapter.

> For everything you say, and for everything you do in a relationship, your partner is going to react to it, especially to your negative remarks and actions.

For the people who like to eat, let me put it another way: There is no free lunch when it comes to your behavior.

You cannot expect to carry out hurtful behavior and give sly insults that are meant to get your point across to him or her and *not* have a negative reaction. They are going to remember it, and they are going to react somehow, some way, at some time.

What types of reactions will they have? Put these on your list for starters: ignoring you, verbally abusing you, cheating on you, hating you, leaving you, not making breakfast for you, or worse, spitting on your French toast when you're not looking. Ouch.

Your partner may have declared unconditional love for you at the wedding day altar, but now he or she must deal with your shit in the trenches of day-to-day life. They are fighting to find happiness, just as you are.

Take it Back! No, You Take it Back!

Let's jump in and begin with the age-old situation in which a lover criticizes the other's appearance. Such a task can be so tricky. Most of us cannot make these comments without getting a negative reaction from our partner. Yes, it is usually less dangerous for women than for men to give this kind of criticism. But having said that, ladies, if you coldly tell your man that his gut is growing and that he better cut down on the beer and pretzels, I can not promise you that that he won't resent your comment. The accumulation of such comments can be fatal to a relationship. So often, the one who is critiquing their partner is also the one who complains and whines that their spouse "just can't get aroused in bed, and I don't know why." I know why: They're too busy thinking about what to do to your French toast.

Men may *appear* to be emotionless beings, but their egos are very sensitive. The reaction to our partner's injustice may not be a vocal argument, and they may even burn our burger when we barbeque, but men also don't forget and don't really forgive. The manifestation of these feelings is aloofness, being limp in the sack, or finding another sack.

After you criticize his or her gut, your partner will probably respond that your stomach is not as flat as a pancake either. Again, you thought you could just casually mention something in passing without getting a negative reaction, but you got slammed, anyway. The result: Now you both feel ugly.

> *It is well established that a woman's sexual arousal with her partner is directly tied to emotional closeness. Men, do NOT forget this when you tell her she's a fat slob.*

Therefore, be careful about what you say and what you do, because there is no taking it back. If you say something inappropriate to your partner, your partner may say to you, "Take that comment back!" Hearing this, you may breathe a secret sigh of relief thinking you can be magically absolved of your sin, but forget it, you can't. Nobody takes anything back once it is out there.

Anyway, It's Your Fault I'm an Idiot

We come into romantic relationships with pre-molded personalities and behaviors. Many of these we have inherited from our parents. If we hear our parents negatively evaluating us with off-the-cuff remarks, furtively critiquing our flaws, we end up doing that same exact thing with our loved ones. Perhaps a parent can get away with imposing these comments on their child because of parent-child bonds, but do not count on this unconditional bond when you're critiquing your spouse's cooking or their failing to get that promotion at work.

We're so ingrained with our own personality that we normally cannot admit to ourselves and to others that we even said something out of line. Our reaction is an innocent, "Well, I didn't mean anything by it. I don't know why you're so upset. And anyway, I'm just trying to help. I was just kidding." Or worse, you have an excuse for making the comment, like being drunk or having had a rough day at the office because your boss invited your co-worker to lunch instead of you.

My favorite devious tactic with my spouse is to turn around and blame *her* for my ugly comment: "I know I should not have said that, but if you weren't so damn late, I would not have been so upset." What I'm really attempting to assert to her—are you ready for it?—that I am merely REACTING to her initial sin, imagined or real.

We have so many excuses for making subtle cuts at our lover and feeling justified for off-hand remarks and actions. But forget it, you're not justified, and you are not going to escape unharmed. Our beloved partner hears everything and is in tune to the messages we convey.

And they are going to get their revenge—one way or another.

My Snowball to You was Thrown Back to Me . . . As an Avalanche

Initial reactions to your actions may be small. Maybe your partner won't talk to you for a while. Maybe they won't feel like buying that bottle of wine to accompany dinner. They may even refuse to make love that night by saying they're too tired.

But as your inappropriate actions grow, their reactions will also grow proportionately destructive until negative reactions become the basis for the relationship. It may go from not having wine to not even dining together. And the sex may go from twice a week to twice every presidential election cycle. And then you wonder, how did we get to this point? Why have I been sleeping in the other bedroom? Why was he or she so mean to go out and find another lover? What did I ever do? I never cheated on her. Why is she acting so damn strange?

Actions by you are never forgotten; they accumulate like a snowball rolling down the mountain into bigger and bigger issues. In most relationships, we even get to the point where we know how the other person is going to react—what their hot buttons are. We know that they will do something like sulk, yell back, or throw a pan at us. Or they may quietly repress their reaction. Quiet repression is probably the most dangerous because we do not *know* they are reacting. As a result, we continue with our destructive actions and words, turning the snowball into a deadly avalanche.

That One Really Hurt

This is not a book on Mars and Venus, but each partner has to realize the perspective of the other. This perspective often revolves around our biological male/female differences. For instance, if the lady says something that is even slightly belittling about the guy's masculinity—yes, pun intended—it can be terribly destructive. Of course, I realize that I am giving you the most lethal weapon you could ever use to get under your man's skin—calling him a sissy. But on the other hand, I am giving you the biggest warning ever that if you do it, your relationship may never ever be the same. The response you receive—the reaction—will be a lack of confidence, and even more aloofness than normal from your man. Every time he kisses you or makes love to you, he may be thinking you don't think he's a real man. Do you really believe the only reason guys can't get it up and need Viagra is because we have clogged arteries?

Conversely, the biggest cutting remark a man can make to a woman is that she is sexually promiscuous. Hints, jokes, sly remarks, and of course, outright insults about her sexual prowess will shut her down faster than a bar after last call.

Each of these killer insults cut to the heart of what we are all about biologically and what the two sexes are sizing each other up on. It sounds corny and old fashioned, but the mating social process still consists of the man testing the woman to make sure that after she has his baby, and he promises to protect her, she will be loyal to him and not stray from the nest. On the other hand, the woman is looking for a protector who is rough and tough enough to keep bad things in the world away from her and her baby. We, therefore, instinctively know that these topics—masculinity for the man and promiscuity for the woman—will always be hot buttons.

How Do I Hate Thee? Let Me Count All the Frickin' Ways!

What's on the list of negative actions and comments? Things like:
- Insults about personal appearance
- Criticisms of the other's workplace
- Family criticisms
- Talking about their mother or father negatively
- Excess spending, substance, or gambling activities
- Lying
- Cheating
- Hitting your lover (whether man or woman)
- Flirting with others
- Neglect

In general, anything can be added to the list of words or actions that would humiliate your partner and will eventually produce a negative reaction.

All these actions create a barrier in which the partners come to believe that they are no longer a unit, but rather, dwelling in a me-against-her environment, and if that's how it's going to be, one or both begin to think, "Maybe I should just live my own life." So many relationships have, at their root, a need by one of the partners to establish power and to control the other. As biological beings, we should not be surprised by this. Isn't it natural to have things our way?

What's worse, though, is that we'll say and do whatever it takes to establish this control. And if that's not enough, after we say and do these things, we then go and find what we think are rational reasons for our actions. For instance, do you really think you're partner would buy this explanation of *your* bad behavior: "I wasn't flirting; we've just been friends for a long time, and I didn't want her to feel like I forgot her." Yeah, right.

Adhere to the old saying, "Think before you act, think before you talk." Try an inner-voice drill before you talk to your partner. Ask yourself: 1) How is she going to react to what I'm about to say or do? Think it through and think what will still be lingering in her mind three days from now. And, also ask yourself: 2) How do I want her to react to what I'm going to say?

The correct answer to both questions for all sexes and orientations should be: My partner will want to have loving but wild sex with me tonight—so much that they'll even be willing to shower beforehand.

Mini Case Study #1

To illustrate, let's say that your wife, a management consultant, had to go on a business trip. And of course, her good-looking male boss went, too, where they worked closely together to win over a new client and probably went to some nice restaurant after work. Also, we'll assume that your wife makes more money than you do. Lots more. She arrives back in town on a Friday afternoon after a successful trip, while you have been home for the last several days washing dirty dishes and watching old reruns of *Modern Family*.

By this point in the narrative, the reader can probably come up with their own smart-ass comment the hubby makes. We'll go with this one: "Nicole, I'm surprised you want to go out to dinner with me after having dinner with your boss all week in a hotel."

Zinger!

Again, just one sentence is enough. Hubby is sensing a loss of control with his successful wife and attempts to reign her in. But what has he done with this one sentence? By mentioning the handsome boss, the pathetic husband has reminded his wife that he feels inferior. Nicole may also be left with the impression that her man is insinuating that her success comes, not from talent and hard work, but simply by using her womanly sex appeal.

What is her reaction to his action? Women readers already know: He's put a damper on dinner—and the entire evening—and perhaps the entire weekend. She may be a cold fish in bed tonight, and, instead of planning fun activities with hubby, she may dismally go through the routines of life, taking little Courtney to gymnastics class and picking up dinner at the food market—and skipping the wine aisle. She will eventually ask herself why should she even try to continue to please her insecure husband or boyfriend; she can go back into work Monday and be appreciated—by her supportive boss.

Women will usually react to hubby's zinger sentence with a frustrated shrug—the first time, and maybe even the fifth time. But their cumulative reaction will be: My husband is indeed inferior to the boss, he thinks little of me, and maybe I should look for someone who is not such a negative drag on me. What does she tell her friend six months later over coffee about why she is now having an affair: "I don't know how it happened, but my husband and I just grew apart."

Forty-one percent of divorced people say they would change their communication style.

Source: Dr. Terri Orbuch, Research Professor, University of Michigan and author of Finding Love Again: 6 Simple Steps to a New and Happy Relationship.

Mini Case Study #2

Do you want to now turn the tables and show an example of a female zinger moment? Let's say that your boyfriend was out drinking with friends and being obnoxious and left you at home watching TV. Upon his return later that evening, you would love to zing him with a remark that magically alters his brain signals so that he does not continue this behavior. Think of a good one. How about this: "Joe, why were you were out drinking last night with Tony and his friends again? You're not, like, secretly attracted to Tony, are you?"

Zinger!

With this one sentence, you *hope* to do three controlling things: 1) make Joe feel guilty about having a good time, 2) stop him from going out without you, and 3) worst of all, make him believe that his girlfriend, you, the most important barometer of his masculinity, questions his manhood.

But what result did you actually achieve? Joe will now resent your trying to take his friends away. He may think that when he is with you, instead of being his choice, it's his obligation. And worst of all, he will have resentment in the bedroom and maybe even lose confidence. How will he regain his confidence? Perhaps by looking for another woman who doesn't question his masculinity.

Moral of the story: when you say something obtuse to your lover, don't be fooled into thinking that your remark will be so clever as to increase your control. Instead, think what he or she is going to do to counteract, not your clever remark, but your obvious attack. Avoid the negative remark or action by thinking of the desired longer term positive outcomes. Like having a nice evening.

Thanks, My BFF Libido—I Owe You One

If you permit me, let us rewind to the lonely husband waiting for his wife to come home from the business trip and pretend that he has enough self-control *not* to make the ill-fated remark. Why would he possibly have such self-control? As it turns out, his own libido deserves the credit. Let's face it. He is going to be pretty horny by Friday night, and even though his brain wants to make the aforementioned stupid insult when she walks through the door, his libido may warn him, "No, you fool, because if you make that pathetic remark now, there's no way you will get any sex tonight." Yes! His libido has thought of the positive outcome, and in doing so, has helped to save the relationship—for now.

But—yes, there is always a *but*—even this outcome could be doomed. Why? Skip ahead, if you will, to our couple lying in bed *after* their libido-freeing excursion into paradise. Let's say it's the next morning, if they could wait that long. Since they just made passionate love, say four times (yes, they really missed each other), he now lays in the bed, exhausted and seemingly libido-satisfied. Ah, but as he lays there and slowly begins to think about breakfast, his thoughts gradually wander back to . . . you guessed it: That slimy boss with the snake eyes. Does hapless husband now make his infamous remark to his wife?

No—Don't do it! Instead, again, think of the future positive outcomes if you do *not* make that stupid remark.

Did I Really Say That?

There may be no sure way to prevent destructive actions. Are we all selfish beings just out for control, willing to say and do anything to increase that control?

As we learned in kindergarten, think before you speak. Not just two seconds before you impulsively blurt some obnoxious gotcha, but two hours before you are in the situation. If you know your wife is coming home this evening from a business trip, what can you say that will have the most positive outcome potential? And, even if your husband comes home late from a night with the boys, use that extra time to create a remark that will be likely to create a positive outcome. It ain't easy, but it ain't impossible, either.

Another way to deal with it is to pretend that everything you say and do in your life is being taped for later playback, to be heard by your mate, your friends, and worst of all, yourself. In these days of ubiquitous technology, it may be true. Would you still do and say what you're doing if it were being taped, later to be played back for public consumption?

If the actions and reactions from your partner become predictably and constantly negative, even after they read this book, then leave the relationship. My father was often a negative reactor. If I were to tell him I just won the big million-dollar lottery, instead of celebrating, he would have probably said, "Oh, hell, you're gonna get killed with income taxes now." Thanks, Dad. Yes, there are lots of negative people in this world, but there are also a good number of positive ones. Look for the positive-reaction people to be in your life.

Our relationships are simply an accumulation of actions and reactions. If the actions are good, then most likely the reactions will be good.

Mom, Close the Damn Door—Please?

How can you prevent yourself from executing destructive comments and actions? What's the test you can give yourself before the venom slips out of your mouth?

One technique to check yourself about being positive in your response is to pretend that you are talking to your mother. Stop and think to yourself: "Would I make this comment and WOULD I USE THIS TONE if I were talking to my mother?" Too often we talk to our lover as if they are a rambunctious school child, especially after we get used to them being around.

If it happens that you never gave your mother any respect, either, then pretend to be talking with your boss. As an example, assume that your spouse, not the neatest person in the world, somewhat carelessly left some papers on the coffee table that you just cleaned off and polished. It's easy to come up with what you'd say to your spouse of 10 years: "Jerry, what the hell do you think you're doing? I just cleaned all this off. Here, take your goddamn papers and get them the hell out of here." I hope that tone strikes you to be at least a little harsh.

Now, how would you ask your boss if she left papers on the conference table? Probably something like this: "Deb, do you want these papers? If you do, I'll put them aside for you on your desk, but if not, I'll just file them with the other old papers, or shall I maybe shred them?"

Quite a difference, huh? Attitude can also be illustrated using the same words. Something as simple as your partner forgetting to gas-up the car. The words to your boss or to your mate may be the same, but I almost guarantee that the tone will be brusque with your mate. "Did you forget to get gas this morning?" Say this sentence once as if you are talking to your stupid spouse. Then go back and say the exact same words as if you asked the same question to your boss or mother. And no cheating when you compare tones.

Practice talking to your mate as if you are talking to your beloved and kindly mother.

You're a Fat Pig Loser—Honey

I can typically tell when couples come into my office how long their marriage will last based on the tone of voice that couples have with each other. Yes, I suppose there could be the couple that, as a natural part of their culture, gripe with each other. There was even an old radio show called "The Bickersons," more commonly referred to as the Bickering Bickersons, who had been married for many years and were famous for their constant arguing. But this was pure fictional entertainment. Again, Hollywood does not translate well into real life.

My client couples who are the happiest, and whose marriages last the longest, talk to each other in a respectful, sweet tone. As I said earlier, they do not belittle each other, they do not talk negatively about their spouse to others, and they give their spouse the benefit of the doubt when there is a debatable question.

In my office, I hear a demeaning tone frequently between spouses. "Harry, why the hell did you bring the wrong papers in?" Then, turning to me, she continues: "He can't get out of his own way. I can't count on him to do anything. I think he's out of his mind half the time."

Or when I am discussing with a couple retirement planning, the man may say, "Jill, why on earth do you still work at that lousy company? They pay you in peanuts and treat you like shit. It's stupid to work there."

I hear these comments and the other partner usually pretends to brush it off. If that is how they talk to each other when out in public meeting with a professional, how do you think they act when alone? I would hope they did not use such a harsh tone when first dating, but we know they probably did. And it's a tone they would not use with people they respect or admire, or certainly with their boss.

So why would you use such a horrible tone with the one you consider the most important person in your life? Too often the answer I hear: "Oh, she's stuck with me (unconditionally), so she doesn't mind." That's what *you* think.

What Would Billy Graham Do?

Absolutely, never, never, ever, ever, use the act of sex with someone else as a revenge reaction against your love mate.

Your partner will never forget it.

You will hope they forgive you. What does forgiveness mean? Does it mean they will forget? Obviously not. Does it mean they will eventually believe you were not wrong? No. Does forgiveness mean they will end up staying with you because of a desire to keep the family unit together, or because the situation that exists is the best the victim can find—for now? Perhaps. If I had to think hard and say what forgiveness is, it's more a state of being, whereby the victim just feels the pain less due to the passing of time. If you're religious, perhaps only God can forgive on Sunday morning what we do on Saturday night. For the rest of us, it takes more time. For a more successful relationship, assume that forgiveness does not exist. It's right up there with unconditional love when we talk about romantic myths.

Before you do something stupid, don't ask yourself if your partner will forgive you. Ask if they will forget what you did. To make the significance of the inflicted scar more realistic, use the operative word forget rather than forgive.

Fact: Flirting is dangerous. Stay focused on your partner, avoiding what you believe are innocent flirtations. Too often, especially with young people, they use it as a control mechanism against their lover, as if to say, "Since you haven't given me what I want, I will go out and associate with others in a way to hurt you." The victim will not forget this, and often react by doing the same thing. Then, suddenly, the relationship is done.

If your partner is flirting, you should tell them you see what they are doing. There is a 110% chance that their response will be denial. After they give a silly or irritated response, just remind them that the focus of the relationship is on the two of you. Say it, even though everyone reading this knows what the flirter's canned response will be: "Of course it is, dear."

It's right and necessary to set rules and boundaries in relationships. Following boundaries will help control some of your destructive actions, and later, reactions. To illustrate: Billy Graham, the late evangelist, reported that he *never* permitted himself to be in a room alone with a member of the opposite sex. That was his boundary rule. What is yours? Be aware, the more loose the boundary, the more doomed the relationship.

Studies show that the likelihood of infidelity is reduced not by going to church on Sunday morning (i.e., claiming to have a moral compass), but rather by reducing the opportunity to do something wrong on Saturday night. It's the same reason we lock our cars: We want to greatly reduce the opportunity for someone walking by to open the door and take something. Said another way: Do not go to first base with someone if you know you should not make it to second base.

Working as an ironworker 40 floors up on the steel frame building of a skyscraper may allow some men to easily adhere to Graham's rule about avoiding contact with the opposite sex. But that's not most men these days. Many work with potential lovers all around. It may be difficult to avoid a one-on-one lunch or even a business trip with such a person. What to do? Set limits! Have lunch or dinner, but don't drink alcohol during the meal or end up at the bar. Don't get up and dance when the music starts. If you need to confer with your colleague, do it in the lobby of the hotel, not your hotel room.

Temptation may be difficult to resist for an older, somewhat bored, married person who suddenly receives attention from a compelling suitor, particularly at work. However, it is even more common for young persons, professional or not, with lots of hormones flowing, who have things going well, so well in fact, that they believe they are immune to the laws of relationships. As a result, they also believe that they can get away with a little fling here and a little tryst there. Don't fall for it. You can't have your cake and eat it forever. The aftertaste is lousy.

Be aware that sexual predators of high rank have a charming way of making younger victims prey to these broken boundaries. Lowlifes like Bill Cosby and Harvey Weinstein set the disgusting standard for this behavior.

A Truly Conditional Reaction

Of course, the ultimate negative action and reaction (besides the funked up French toast) is the act of sexual infidelity. Many cheaters believe that they can cheat, get caught, repeatedly deny they were cheating, and then ask for their partner's forgiveness. The cheaters seem sincere in their plea: "Look, honey, it was a mistake. But it was just one time and it's over. Let's move on and forget it."

Let's be clear: The cheated-on partner is *not* going to forget about it. No way. No how. Not 'til the cows come home. Not even after you win the Powerball Lottery. You can buy her or him as many "How to Forgive" books that are published, but your partner will still not forgive you. If you're lucky, they will live with it. And they will get their revenge.

In my more than 30 years of working with couples, I have never seen a relationship that was ever the same after infidelity.

The victimized spouse will be colder, more aloof, continue to be more resentful, even if they stay with their partner. That's why, when a public figure is caught cheating, our favorite pastime is observing the spouse's reaction to the nightmare. It's especially juicy when the cheater drags the spouse to the podium to witness the mea culpa plea. "Yes, I made a mistake," he says solemnly, "but we are working things out."

Unconditional Love Sucks!

One of the best examples on YouTube is that of former New York Governor Elliot Spitzer's resignation press conference as his wife stands next to him—after he was caught having an affair with a high-priced prostitute. You gotta' love how he talks about healing himself and his family and moving toward ideals that lead to hope.

"Sure, I forgive the bastard."

Are Spitzer and his wife still together? After 26 years of marriage, and 5 years after the scandal, she finally divorced him—the ultimate reaction. And got millions, too.

TIP: Add to your wedding vows that you will be courteous to each other. I never see this done, but it becomes of paramount importance in our day-to-day togetherness.

TIP WITHIN A TIP: Post your wedding vows with a magnet right on your fridge door, so you can be reminded of them every day.

Bring your best behavior and attitude to the relationship. Constantly and unconditionally. Indeed, it's the only part of a relationship that should be unconditional. If you do not bring your best game, you might as well move on to a new partner, because if you don't, your current lover probably will.

Chapter 7

The Sex Chapter

"When a Marriage Goes on the Rocks, the Rocks Are There, Right There!", Big Mamma Declares as She Points to a Big Brass Bed.
—Cat on a Hot Tin Roof, 1955

Why You're on the Bottom—Statistically, That Is.

I find it fascinating that a recent survey called people and asked if they had sex the day before. How would you like to work for that survey company? For the people who responded yes, only 25% of this group indicated that the sex included any extensive romantic foreplay. That means that 75% of you are jumping in bed or on the couch and doing it, and then you are done. That amazes me in this day-and-age—in any day or age. What is it with you 75%ers?

> *Do you really believe your partner is going to continue to love you unconditionally if you do not give them good sex? Unless there is a major physical disability, and you think this way, you are living in fantasy land, and by necessity, so is your spouse.*

I did not review any further details of the findings, but I would *love* to know what is going on in your minds as to why there is so little foreplay before finishing off. There is something really wrong there—you are missing out on some really fun and satisfying experiences.

You can read all kinds of surveys about the reasons for divorce, but the sex and intimacy thing always ends up being a major factor in a break-up. I've *never* had a client come in to talk divorce and tell me: "Yeah, we have a great sex life, but you know, we just can't agree on TV shows, so I want to dump the loser." Never. I more commonly hear: "We haven't had sex for a year and a half, except one time when we were really drunk."

It's understandable that each of us has different sexual appetites, but the not-so-obvious conclusion from this fact: one of the partners believes that they are not getting their fair share—and believe me, it's not always the man who may feel short-changed.

I'm no sex therapist, but I've been around long enough to know what's at work to create the 75%ers. Here's my shot at it:

1. Are you binging on Netflix instead of each other?

We've all heard that people are tired at the end of the day, and they watch TV, and then fall asleep while watching TV, probably on the couch or in bed. Don't fall into this trap. The alternative is to plan your sex earlier, say right after dinner—or during dinner?!—and to get rid of the TV in your love chamber. Studies have shown that a television in the bedroom is a sex killer. The evening routine of dinner, dinner clean-up, kids' homework, television, then dozing off to sleep, is a perfect recipe for the 75% finding. If the Game of Thrones is too irresistible, plan a sex date for Saturday or Sunday morning—even if you have to miss Face the Nation or book a hotel for three hours to escape the dog and kiddies.

And speaking of kids, if you have little ones, get them to bed early—and make sure that it is their bed and not yours—so you have private time. I have seen more than one marriage end up in counseling because one of the spouses dotes on the children more than their partner. With working couples, many parents feel guilty about not being with their child during the day, and to compensate for this situation, essentially ignore their lover in the evening.

Warning: If you dedicate more effort to your children than your partner, such action will ricochet in a nasty reaction.

---

2. Are you getting enough stimulation to get those good vibrations?

If you are going to have a TV in the bedroom, use it to play a little porn. No matter your religion or moral ethics, some fun porn always livens up the sex. And guys, be aware, that porn is as much, if not more, of a turn-on for the ladies than it is for you. Porn is especially good for people who have been in a long-term relationship. Leave your morals at the church or in temple. I don't care if you go to church seven days a week and you have never said "shit" in your life, when you get in the sack, don't be Mother Teresa.

And, never be judgmental with your lover or their past trysts. There's an old joke in which one person tells his partner that she has the most beautiful breasts in the world. When she slaps him and he is stunned at her reaction, she declares, "That was for knowing the difference."

Don't forget the toys—to be used with each other, not alone. These days, you can buy them at Walgreens. If you have just started being intimate with a partner, I know you're probably a big horn ball and may not need them much. That's OK, too.

3. Are you clean enough to be dirty?

This is a big one but often hard to execute. Take account of when you shower or bathe. Are you an evening or morning bather? I find it amazing that most people shower in the morning so that they look fresh and clean for the people at work, many of whom they may not even like very much. Meanwhile, they go to bed without bathing after a full day of perspiration, smelly restaurants, and taking the trash out. After you've been up all day doing grimy things and then retire for the evening, you are not only getting the sheets dirty and smelly, do you really expect to have your partner turned on by your stinky armpits—and other pits? That's UL above and beyond the call.

Good news for the British reader: It's been found that most people in your country sleep in the nude. The bad news: The English change sheets only four times a year. And they shower in the morning!

I know most people do not shower both in the evening and morning—unless you're newly dating or maybe a workout nut. For those of us in long-term relationships, the combination of, well, a long-term relationship, with an unhygienic body is a recipe for lousy sex or no sex at all.

4. Hair should be a show on Broadway, not a jungle to machete through in your bedroom.

As I said before—and if I didn't, I should have—for any part of your body that will probably be kissed, squeezed, stroked, licked, or sniffed, you probably need to do one very important thing besides wash it clean: shave it. Your partner does not want to get involved in a hairy mess. Perhaps for a novelty or to show you are macho or an exotic amazon woman, a temporary journey into hairiness may provide a varied experience for your partner. But it's really off-putting to think you will need a bobby pin to find what you're looking for. Not to mention that awkward moment when in the heat of battle, you pause to remove that annoying piece of hair in your mouth: "Honey, wait a minute, my tongue definitely feels a hair floating around in my mouth; just give me a minute to find the damn thing and get rid of it." Right. Luckily for men, I hope the shaving thing does not include our chest hair—unless you women tell me otherwise.

5. Do you really want to hear the bad news now?

Sex is better when people look better, not just smell better and have shaved. So, look good for your partner. And you look good for your lover when you are in good health.
If you are fit, you will be sexier for your spouse. If your spouse is fit, he or she will seem sexier to you. And when you're both sexier, the two of you will want to do more things together—in and out of the bedroom.
And I realize that Kim Kardashian, a major sex symbol—or some kind of symbol— is two devil dogs away from being in this dangerous territory as well. If she can fight temptation and stay fit, we can too, damn it.

Unconditional Love Sucks!

No butts about it, you can look like Kim K, too.

Exercise and watching your diet is a pain. I know. However, if you exercise, you will feel more confident about yourself and also about your physical ability to wrestle around in bed. For the man, exercise also increases the testosterone levels which increases your libido. It will probably also delay the need for erectile dysfunction medicine. You know, the blue pills.

Don't be afraid to start your exercise program small and slow. On day one, do only one sit-up, or even just a half of one. The next day, double it to one. Then, the next day, do two. See, that doesn't sound so bad, does it? But in just three days, you have quadrupled the number of sit-ups you can do. Try the same technique for pushups, running or even walking. Take little steps, then increase them.

And if you think you don't have the space in your place, simply slide that bedroom bureau more into the corner to give you a little more room. No need to go to the gym—until you're ready to show off. Some couples may want to embark on this mission as a team. Fine, but still do it at your own individual pace.

More bad news: As my friends and I age, and we fail to stay fit, we may become physically unable to have sex, even if we manage to shave our entire body. Physical fitness sins in our thirties and forties, like drinking too much, eating lots of pizza with pepperoni, and driving pass the gym, catch up with us, and result in things like bad knees, painful hips, and erectile dysfunction. Try to stay fit. There are many long-term benefits that you may not think about when you're young and careless.

75% of lovers just have perfunctory sex and fall asleep. What do the five suggestions above have in common? They take extra effort. Tackle these issues and become a 25%er.

Oh, It's You Again

Another consequence of couples getting tired of each other and taking the other for granted: Less sex—at least with each other.

Almost as bad as drifting to other lovers, and even lazier, is the solution of having more sex—with yourself. Be careful guys; Save your hormones and other fluids for your partner. But it's so convenient, you say! There's no need to shave, shower, or even be nice. Just resort to your go-to adult website, and maybe the toy stashed in the drawer, and you're all set. You think, "I can stink, drink, and fight with my mate—and still have sex!"

Yeah, sort of. Remember that in the previous chapter we talked about how for every action (or lack thereof) by you, there is a reaction from you-know-who.

Oh, yes, I am talking to you, ladies, as well, here. If your best friend is your vibrator, you need to probably step up your game, or find a game elsewhere.

Ladies—and men—you don't want your partner telling the following joke at the bar after work: Why do priests practice celibacy? So they can relate to their married parishioners.

You're a Jerk—Now Let's Make Love

Remember, ladies, that like you, men have sensitive egos. You can't insult and belittle them during the day and then expect to have great sex later that night. Guys have to feel good about ourselves and believe that you feel good about us, too, especially when we're in a longer-term relationship. If a woman rejects sex because it's her period or has that classic headache, the guy will quietly go into the bathroom with his cell phone and turn on the most convenient free porn site. Yes, for every action there is a reaction. Give clear signals, and make an extra effort to your partner that you are willing, ready and able. Taking that shower in the evening, wearing your fishnet stockings, not looking totally engrossed while you watch Housewives of Atlanta.

Women have to help the guys. And even tell them what to do.

Studies have shown that school students do better in a subject if they are told that they excel in a subject. In fact, they will even sign up for more difficult subjects if there is reinforcement about their success. The same holds for sexual performance, and it goes to my point about instilling confidence in the other partner. If you complain to the other partner that they're no good in the sack, they are not going to have the confidence to enjoy you, let alone try things more adventurous.

I love the part in the film *Annie Hall* where we simultaneously see each partner through split screen in separate counseling sessions with their respective shrinks. Woody Allen's character tells his shrink that he and Annie *hardly* have sex anymore, maybe just three times a week. The camera then cuts to the other half of the screen where girlfriend Annie tells her shrink that she doesn't know what her partner's problem is, that he wants to have sex *too* much: "even three times a week." I love that scene because it's the stereotype of the Mars-Venus difference between partners that we always believe gets in the way of relationships.

If you get a partner who is very shy, cautious, and conservative with sex, and your reaction is to make less of an effort to be creative and giving in bed, you may think that's the end of it, but you are wrong. Your love mate has a mind and body of sexuality that is brimming under the surface, and if you think it is not there, you are fooling yourself.

Surveys have shown that action between the sheets is just as important—if not more—for women as it is for men. We certainly know that women can have more orgasms than men. So, do not underestimate the sexuality of a woman. I recently saw on a Spanish-speaking television station a mature Latin woman declare that men and women are different because sex is not as important to the woman. Wrong! Men should erase that theory from their minds. If men assume that, the relationship will slip from one of romance to one of business, and unfortunately, most business relationships fail.

Did it Improve Michael Jackson's Sex Life?

I haven't had any plastic surgery—yet—so I may not be an authority on this. But since you've come this far, you might as well keep reading. Most people I have talked to, and who have talked to me, have told me that it gives them more confidence. And if you have more confidence, you'll probably be better in bed. You just have to be careful of limits. I realize we have seen so many celebrities go out of control with over-doing such procedures. We ask ourselves why they went so far. If they don't know when to stop, are you going to know when *your* limit is reached?

You probably can't ask your friend or lover about when you are approaching plastic surgery limits. Friends may be a little jealous, or you think they are. Unless it is extremely extreme, even the plastic surgeon may not be objective because he is looking more closely at his bank account than your tired chin. You can't ask your mother for an opinion, because she does not want to see you suffer under the surgeon's knife—plus she may feel bad that your surgery is having to correct her genetic flaws passed on to you!

Ideally, ask someone at your work place of the opposite sex whom you have known some time, but someone who will believe that if he or she is frank with you, there is little to lose in a relationship. Do not ask your boss or a subordinate—you want no sexual harassment issues with this thing.

Come to think of it, the first surgery is probably going to be your call. Maybe the person in the office is the one to ask when getting your *second* plastic surgery—or the dreaded, but all too common do-over.

What happens if you get the plastic surgery and it does not increase your love life? Then don't get the second one. The problem may not be your appearance. Just ask Michael Jackson.

Unconditional Love Sucks!

The King of Pop at his limit?

What do tattoos, plastic surgery, and potato chips have in common? You can't stop at just one. Think!

J. A. Dougherty

Chapter 8
The Money Chapter
Or One Bed, Two Banks

"I truly believe that women should be financially independent from their men."

—Beyoncé

Unconditionally Broke

Finances and money are a central ingredient to problems surrounding the myth of unconditional love.

Many of you inherently believe that your unconditional marriage includes your partner's unconditional promise to financially be there for you. If our divorce rate is about 50%, are you willing to flip that coin and hope that it will financially fall heads up for you? The myth of UL is a luxury that may financially break you.

Let's look at the dollars and sense of it. We face a cruel, cruel retirement world today in that we cannot depend on our employers to create a magical pension fund for us. We must do it all ourselves. If having to come up with all of our own retirement savings were not difficult enough, once we stash the money away, the growth rate on our savings is often unpredictable. The only way our retirement plans are going to grow is if *we continue to make regular contributions to savings.* Year after year, month after month, and week after week.

Even worse, many couples try to compensate for the failure of expectations not being met (happiness not achieved) in other areas of the marriage by spending more money on each other. Whether out of love or laziness, they spend more money and continue to do so, then start borrowing money, until they are broke. Be very careful that you do not express your love or attempt to satisfy the other's expectations by spending money that you do not have.

Here's an extreme but very real example: New Jersey TV housewife Teresa Giudice. What on earth got into her mind to be sucked up into her husband's financial and fraudulent nightmare? It's obviously a combination of many elements, but one of the major factors was a complacent attempt by Teresa to satisfy her husband's screwy financial expectations. As a result, they ended up bankrupt and doing time in prison.

"My mug shot is cooler than yours." "Yeah, but I had a better hair day."

Separate, But Not Always Equal

This tendency to spend as a desire for happiness is a reason I advocate separate finances for married and cohabitating couples, especially if both work. It is easier to stay focused on financial goals when each can manage their own money. I know—this contradicts virtually every book on couples financial planning that you'll read.

Unconditional Love Sucks!

> ***News Bulletin:*** *I find that spouses and partners are most successful with finances when they keep their finances separate. Yes, I know we have all heard that since the time couples first lived together in the same cave they should share finances, including one checking account, jointly owned homes and cars, and both names on the credit cards. But we don't live in caves anymore.*
> [Read the Beyoncé quote at the the head of this chapter]

Separate finances include maintaining individual banking, investment, and especially credit card accounts. The IRS already requires that our retirement accounts, such as IRAs and 401Ks, be kept in individual names. What have they known for so long that we do not?

Have you heard the one about two realtors who have wild sex on their first date? Do you know what they do on their second date? Buy property together. Probably a big mistake.

And it's not just realtors.

Consider buying houses, furniture, and toys—and this time I'm not talking about the ones that vibrate, but rather those that ride and float—in individual names, not jointly. Why? With individual ownership comes the understanding that possession will follow the owner if there is a break-up. In common-law marriage states (each state differs), this arrangement may require a written agreement between parties to identify respective ownership. *

> ** Common law states include Alabama, Colorado, District of Columbia, Iowa, Kansas, Montana, New Hampshire, Oklahoma, Rhode Island, South Carolina, Texas, Louisiana, and Utah. For older relationships, Georgia, Idaho, Louisiana, New Hampshire, Pennsylvania may also be in this group.*

Does having separate assets and a written agreement seem too *unromantic*? Just the contrary. By having separate ownership, you and your lover are saying, "I and my possessions are here with you, not because I'm required by some joint ownership structure, but because I want to be here."

The point of this entire book is about bringing self-responsibility to the success of your relationship, without the burden of false unconditional love or the complacency that leads to secret grudges and resentments. No tool for this partnership self-responsibility can be better utilized than smart financial management.

> *Many divorced singles say that "money was the number one source of conflict in the early years of marriage," and that "six out of ten said they would not share living expenses in their next relationship." Source: Dr. Terri Orbuch, Research Professor at the University of Michigan and author of "Finding Love Again: 6 Simple Steps to a New and Happy Relationship."*

Too many couples, however, don't save enough, spend too much, and of course, end up blaming the other partner for their financial problems. When you keep things separate, there is a natural system of checks and balances. If one spouse is spending too much, then you know where to focus on the problem. There is no blame game. Are you listening, Teresa and Joe?

Having things separate can also create a healthy competition (the ONLY area I recommend for competition in a romantic relationship) to spend wisely and save a lot. Each of you can set a goal for savings. All this is true for married as well as live-together partners. Too often I find boyfriend-girlfriend, boyfriend-boyfriend, girlfriend-girlfriend, deciding as soon as they live together, to share finances—they want to nest. They make it official that they are playing house by having a joint checking account. With nesting comes buying the puppy dog, eating the popcorn while watching *Bridgerton* on the used sofa, and of course, opening the joint checking account. Then, a little later, you'll want to buy the house together and even the vacation home.

As time goes on, there is less money in the bank, and credit card debt has accumulated. It is ironic that many couples I see do better with money *after* they are divorced, despite the conventional wisdom about crippling alimony expense and financially abandoned spouses. (With improved income earning opportunity, and having children later, many women are able to save more for retirement single than if married.)

As marriage conventions change, financial effects are noticeable, too. Upon this writing, even the IRS is evolving away from spousal relationships. When they send a collection notice out to taxpayers, they send a notice out to each spouse individually. When I represent a married couple before the IRS related to a joint tax return, the IRS requires separately signed forms by each spouse giving me their power of attorney. It's almost as if the IRS is declaring: We don't know who is married, who is not married, but if your name is on the return, we're coming after you.

Let me tell you a little about my own experience. During my first marriage, we had joint everything, including joint poverty. My now ex-wife had a debit card and of course she always needed cash. This was the same account with which we would write checks to pay bills. You guessed it: There was never any money in the account when it came time for those bills to be paid. We made good income, but spent everything and saved nothing. Even though we had a joint account, I did not know what she was spending money on because of the cash ATM withdrawals. Of course, all of that was good reason for arguing and building resentments.

Now fast-forward to my current marriage in which we have come into the relationship with our separate assets and income, and, to some degree, our own expenses. We have agreed—and tried—to keep everything separately titled. We have separate wills, our own trusts, and we have separate checking and credit card accounts. We also agreed which one of us is responsible for paying each of the household expenses. One of us pays the electric, one pays the property taxes, one of us generally pays when we go to a restaurant, etc.

As a result, there is very little to argue about when it comes to money. We also do not have the other person to blame if we are broke this month. If we believe that something is too expensive, we discuss the issue, then cry a little. Of course, we can still find ourselves getting into the trap of spending too much to please the other person on things like vacations and gifts. We solve this problem by having preplanned budgets for those big items. If we go to Europe this year, we cannot afford to go next year. We agree that our holiday gift budget will be $_____ per person this year.

I am able to save money as never before. And my ex-wife tells me she manages money better now as a single. Go figure.

I am actually a big proponent of keeping separate checking accounts for each partner. This is especially true if each spouse works. Come to an agreement about who pays for such things as the utilities, mortgage, and similar common expenses. When each person has their own checking account, then their expectations are more defined and more reigned in. Also, if you have your own credit cards, if one spouse decides to split the scene for good, it is more difficult for them to destroy the credit—and run up the balance—against the deserted partner. And vice versa. Over the years, I have seen this more times than I can count.

When one of the lovers leaves a relationship, the other tells me, naively, that "he took the joint credit card with him, but I don't think he would be mean enough to take advantage of the situation." Then, a week later, they return to my office to report that the credit card balance is run up to the $5,000 limit, and guess who is expected to pay it off. If the payments are not made, credit scores are severely tarnished.

Banks, of course, will want both spouses to sign for loans. Why? So, they have more people on the hook. Obviously, this is an incentive not to get legally married, and it is one of the unfair laws that exist for married couples. I discuss this whole issue of legal marriage in chapter 13, because it not only relates to legal fairness, it is plays into the myth of unconditional love.

Too often I've seen live-together couples sign up for joint credit cards only to have one of them turn out to be an uncontrollable spender. And speaking of signing on as a guarantor of a loan, there is a high statistical chance that the guarantor will eventually be on the hook for the loan of the deadbeat partner.

Let the partner get the loan for his car, and you get a separate loan for your car—individually—even if the salesman says that you will get a lower rate if both are co-signers for the loan. Unlike a house mortgage, a car loan is much less in value and duration, and therefore, giving up a few points of interest makes little difference in the big picture of personal financial planning.

I do not have enough fingers and toes to count the number of times a credit rating of one partner has been damaged by the actions of the other partner, married or not, but more often married. Why? Because they are trying to keep the other partner happy by attempting to satisfy expectations. Or, they did not know that their partner was a compulsive spender.

Speaking of credit ratings, if you are using a checklist of qualifiers for future partners, you might as well find out his or her credit score. Of course, you can't say, while administering a gentle back massage, "Honey, can you shoot me a copy of your credit rating by lunchtime tomorrow, because I really don't trust your ass?" But, perhaps start off by mentioning your own credit score and some of the problems you may have had with inaccuracies, etc. Then go in for the kill: "Honey bun, do you know what your credit score is?" If they do not give an absolute specific number—who can?—advise him or her that it's in their best interest to review their credit report from time to time to avoid fraud, and best of all, you will help them print it out. Credit card companies, banks, and even auto insurance companies review these reports. Why shouldn't you, especially if you are going to purchase assets together.

An important note: even though I advocate separate accounts and separate management of finances for couples, if you are considered legally married, remember that most states will consider all these assets marital property if acquired during your marriage. (For more details, Google search the rules for your state.) What does it mean if it is a marital asset? Upon divorce, even in common law marriage states, those assets will be considered to be owned 50/50 by each spouse in evaluating spousal allocation. This includes checking accounts, IRA and 401K accounts, homes, cars, and that original Picasso you bought on your honeymoon in Vegas. The only assets that may be excluded are those identified in a prenuptial agreement or those inherited or brought into a marriage at the beginning. But if you and your spouse have accumulated assets during a marriage, and certainly commingled such assets (for example, by living for 10 years together in a house inherited or gifted from Dad), it is probably a 50/50 marital asset. I say this because when

I give clients advice about maintaining separate assets, the partner with the weaker finances often worries—I can actually see the look on their face—about losing out if a split occurs later.

If your partner is overly concerned that the assets are not joint, re-examine his or her true expectations in the relationship. Is it love or money? Proposing the separation of assets and expenses alone may be a good test for the likelihood of long-term success. (If you are afraid to suggest this, just blame the idea on this crazy book.)

What happens if only one spouse works? Do we have just one joint account? Even then I would suggest having a second account for the non-working spouse and agree on what gets spent from this second account for some expenses (e.g., family food, spouse's gas, and entertainment), and give that partner a generous range of control to spend—or save—as they wish.

The plethora of real-life horror stories I've witnessed is the reason I write this book. Couples buy property and then break up. More times than not, one of the individuals believes they were taken advantage of by the other person. That is, she ends up believing that there was some premeditated profit motive to go in jointly with a purchase so that he could end up with a piece of the assets after the break-up.

One unmarried couple I knew came up with a screwy idea to buy an expensive recreational vehicle they could not afford. The one who really wanted the RV didn't have the money to buy it, so the other partner had to put up the money—and sign up for the debt as the guarantor. When things when from bad to worse, they both had to file for bankruptcy.

Another couple I know had a situation in which the husband, we'll call Jerk, asked his high-income wife, whom we'll call Pushover, to buy an expensive pleasure boat for the two of them. Pushover came up with the money to purchase the cruiser from a neighbor, but just one day—yes, one day—after the purchase, Jerk claimed the boat was not acceptable and returned it to the neighbor for a cash refund. And guess what? Jerk kept the cash for himself, and I mean thousands of dollars that his wife never saw again!

A Dirty Word We All Hate: Budgeting

First, as I've said earlier, let me tell you what I do not like: debit cards. Joint debit cards can be poison, especially if there is little communication between you. Too often, before you know it, the account is negative, and there is nothing left to pay the electric bill. That's because one or both of you have been hitting the debit card. Debit cards also make it difficult to track where the money is going. So, if you have lots of budget problems or can't make your money last until the end of your pay period, reconsider how you use your debit cards. The first step is to identify where the money is going. It is hard, ordinarily, because, with a debit card, a little money goes here, and a little goes there, and by the end of the month it adds up to a lot of zero in your account.

With budgets, the less money you have access to, the better. This is another reason for separate accounts between partners.

By the way, having separate accounts does not mean that they have to be secretive, unless the owners of the account wish them to be. In my case, I normally do not look at my wife's checking account balance, nor does she look at mine. It's one less thing each of us has to worry about.

The only thing I like about debit cards is that they can be used like a credit card but without the building up of debt; when it takes money out of your checking account, the money is gone, but you have not accumulated a balance due later. In this sense, I would rather you use this than a credit card, but carefully!

Don't use the lack of clever accounting as an excuse for spending too much. If you can't save, then you need to see where you are spending the money. (And you may need to get a second job!)

I know people who make $50,000 per year that can save $10,000, and I know others that make a half million who cannot save a dime. Amazing.

> *In addition to separate bank accounts, I recommend that you have funds regularly withdrawn from your pay or checking account to put away for savings. Money never seen is money not missed. Somehow you will survive.*

Tell your bank or your employer or your broker to start slicing out 50 or 100 bucks per week or month. And don't think of this money as a source for date night or the Hawaiian cruise. The money is locked away; you can't touch it. If you want to deposit these funds to a traditional or Roth IRA, that's even better. Call a company like Vanguard or TD Ameritrade for assistance in the mechanics.

Opposites may attract physically, but from what I've seen in my office, they go crazy when dealing with each other's finances. If you have one that is concerned about overspending and the other that's not, they are both going to drive each other crazy. On the other hand, if neither is concerned about overspending, the road to ruin usually ends in bankruptcy. I have seen it as a major conflict area. Does it usually end in divorce? Not as a rule, from my observation. I know one couple in which the husband loves to spend too much, gamble, go broke, then move to a new town so he can start all over again. The wife just keeps tagging along with him. In fact, I've heard that she'll even hide and destroy those bothersome incoming bills so that he doesn't get too stressed out. Now that's a sympathetic—or enabling—wife.

Can I Just Pay You Cash?

Fully 20% of our adult population doesn't even have a checking account. Those people are using a full cash system to pay bills and expenses. Even if you have a checking account, you may want to use a hybrid cash method to budget monthly expenses. The method I refer to also has been called the envelope system, whereby on payday, you line up several envelopes on the kitchen table. Each envelope represents a separate category of expense, such as food or entertainment or gasoline. You place your budgeted cash for each category into its respective envelope, and that is your allowed expense until the next pay period. I know it's easier said than done; you may stop by the local grocery store and happen not to have your food envelope with you. But, for the people who have used this method, it seems to work. When the money in the envelope runs out, you have run out of money for that expense category for that period.

More Fun than Budgeting: Setting Goals

When managing your finances, it's very important to have written goals. I'm not talking about small goals like whether your next car is blue or red, but rather big lifetime goals that will make a difference in your long-term future. Establish a goal to achieve in just one year and a second goal to be reached in five years. For example, by the end of this year, I will put away $10,000. In two-years I am going to have a better job. In five years, I am going to be living in Hawaii. Have it written, have it posted on the fridge, and have it committed to by you *and* your partner.

By not having shared written goals, it too often creates a situation of unidentified expectations and dreams unfulfilled.

Life goals include desired job positions, education attainment, amount of money in the bank, vacation destinations, retirement account contribution rates, living arrangements/location, how much to save for children's goals.

A word about saving for children. Too many people I have worked with over the years have lived and diluted their savings through their children. And too often, they end up miserable and financially strapped. Give your child the upbringing so they may catch their own fish and not take the ones you caught.

Don't hesitate to meet with a financial advisor to develop major goals and strategies. It is unfortunate that the ones who should do this, do not. This phenomenon is similar to what college administrators find: Those students who seek academic advice are usually the better students who really don't need much advice, and conversely, the students struggling never come in for help. I find the same thing with adults and couples seeking financial counseling. I do not know if it's because they are just born worriers, but my most successful clients are in the office reviewing their investment, estate, and life strategies, while the people who are in debt and broke, who could really benefit from third-party input, hardly come in to see me.

For you movers and shakers, I also like the idea of meeting with someone at home or at a comfortable retreat for several hours every couple years to brainstorm planning ideas, then summarizing focused strategy implementation objectives. Common components:

1. Goals
2. Challenges to accomplishing goals
3. Interim tasks required to accomplish goals
4. Person responsible for task
5. Completion dates of tasks

After the meeting, keep these summarized plans visible to you—yes, even by the mirror used for applying make-up in the morning.

I knew one consultant who used to facilitate such meetings—with high powered individuals who called such planning sessions their biennial dump. His clients would dump out ideas, complaints and fears as they formulated and updated a set of goals and tasks for their lives. These were high-level, high-achievement people. It was worth it for them to pay a few thousand dollars for this individual session because of the significant benefits.

One of secrets to the facilitator's success is his request to spread the meeting over two days. He meets initially with his client on day one in the afternoon, then breaks for the evening to digest the session. When they reconvene the next morning, they review the salient points of the previous day to confirm or discount ideas developed. Upon confirmation of goals and objectives, they work on specifics of tasks, challenges and timelines.

By the time the client and facilitator end the final session, they have formulated the direction of the client's life for the next couple of years and the specific goals to pursue. Do not underestimate how powerful this process is.

Who's the Boss, Anyway?

The process my consultant friend works with is also a wonderful technique to be used by love partners to define expectations for themselves as a "team." On a more day-to-day basis, spouses who work together in a business or some professional project should separate their work time from their companionship time. Develop boundaries and compartmentalize. Have a physical work office or designated clock schedule that identifies when you are in work mode and when you are not. If you do not work professionally together, but have a business-like project, such as contracting to build a new custom house, have a board meeting at your kitchen table to discuss project issues. By identifying discussion as a board meeting, you can talk directly about business issues, even disagree, and not worry—I hope—about being offended by frank comments.

You also choose a meeting adjournment time. After the meeting is over, you leave the business issues and resume your romantic companionship. You must agree—and this is the most important part—not to discuss the project any other time. Not over dinner, not tucking yourselves into bed later that night. If you need further discussions, have another board meeting.

When my wife and I were building our home, the general contractor went broke and ran out on us when the house was about 75% complete. We were now the general contractor and had to hire and supervise the carpenters, plumbers, and half the town's trade workers, in addition to making sure we had proper permitting and compliance with the home owners' association. It was a nightmare! We would have tried couple counseling to survive this trauma, but it was no longer in our budget. Instead, we had board meetings every night between five and six to review progress and determine whom we had to call, hire and fire the next day.

But after the board meeting finished (that is, after we argued about every issue), there was no more discussion about this topic until the next meeting. Letting these issues torment us 24 hours a day could have killed our love chemistry. The five o'clock meetings saved our sanity and our relationship.

The board-meeting method does not just have to be used with building your new home. Vacations, new cars, children's education, and other major planning tasks can be nicely accommodated for these sessions. I have especially seen it work well in family-run businesses, too, which can be difficult, especially if spouses are working together. You should define when it's business time, and when business time is done. If you work together all day, and I see it more frequently now with spouses working at home in virtual offices, it can be difficult to avoid each other. I am a big advocate of leaving the business at the business. My most successful clients have made sure they make this segregation.

Maybe in Sickness and Health, but Probably Not . . .

I don't necessarily believe the statistic cited earlier about money being a major source of couples' conflict. Is it about money or expectations? If most problems arise from financial difficulties, millionaires would never divorce. But they do. Obviously, there are other expectations, that is, other conditions, that are not being met. And perhaps the issue related to money—whether we are rich or poor—is just one more item on the list.

As with your appearance, your habits and your behavior, bring your best to your partner, too, in the area of managing money. Believe it or not, your lover will not always be there if you expect them to put up with your financial irresponsibility. If you are counting on the "For better, for worse, for richer, for poorer" delusion to make your partner tolerate you, remember that nobody wants to be unconditionally broke all their life—especially if there are other piggy banks in the pig pen.

Chapter 9
Modern Men, Women, and Other Genders

*"A strong woman can do everything herself.
A strong man is there so she doesn't have to."*

—B. De Loere

All Aboard!

The idea that we must question Unconditional Love is all that more important as the roles of men and women evolve in our changing society. In the past, if a homemaker wife were more or less stuck with an abusive husband—yes, a jerk—females had little choice but to buy the UL crap. They were told, "He's far from perfect, honey, and your life is a miserable cesspool, but it will be worse if you leave him." For many women in such a dismal predicament, that train has left the station, and does not—should not—imprison them any longer. Not only has the train left the station, today many women are the engineers driving it.

Over the last several years, the public roles of women and men have been changing. Women have taken on more of a leadership presence in the work force and other areas. They have been expanding into careers that were once largely dominated by men. Women have been taking on management and other high-level positions. It has become normal to expect that many young females will go on to higher education and enter important careers.

Fun Facts About Changing Times
- In 1960, 60% of 29-year-olds were married.
- In 2015, only 20% of 29-year-olds were married.

- Today, a mere 16% of 18 to 29-year-olds are married.
- Another 14% of 18 to 29-year-olds are cohabitating with a partner.

- The median age to get married from 2016 data: 27
- For the previous 100 years, the median age to marry was between 18 and 22.

- Over half of the U.S. population are currently *not* married.
- Half of births to women under age 30 are from unmarried women.

- More single women than single men are buying homes.
- Women born after 1990 drink as much alcohol as men their same age—a milestone since records have been kept.

(Sources: June 2016 Gallup poll; U.S. Bureau of Labor Statistics; *Big Girls Don't Cry* by Rebecca Traister)

Increasingly, women's achievements are prominent. Females have taken their skills in nurturing, intuition, and family organization to the workplace, combining them with technical and management training. Women will continue to make strides, and we should all hope for this.

Excuse Me, Where Can I Find the Men's Dorm?

On the other hand, the position of the male has become somewhat more tenuous in society. I do not believe in a zero-sum game for the sexes, meaning that if women advance professionally, she will get the job at the expense of men. But in the last generation, the female has certainly shown her superior skills in many fields. In 2022, Women in Academia (WIA) report that 55.6% of all first year medical school students are female. For law school, the rate is about the same, 55.7%. Contrast this to just 55 years ago when only 3.7% of law school students were women. The report also indicates that close to one-third of law school deans are now women. Finally, according to data from the Department of Education, for every 74 males graduating college, 100 females will graduate—and that's old data from 2019.

An unfortunate result of these developments is that many men are intimidated by the upward mobility of the modern female. One young man says he is interested in a particular lady, but will not ask her out, because, why would *she*, a pre-law student, go out with a measly accounting major? I call it gender career intimidation.

When I talk to young women, many of them exude a confidence—and some a smugness—that they will have plenty of opportunity over time to choose a suitable partner. Of course, this confidence is derived in part from their academic accomplishments combined with a belief in strong career opportunities.

Ironically, as a result of the elevated economic success of women, both sexes are often finding themselves in a bind. Even though females may be confident of more resources to attract an acceptable mate, the opposite may be true: Women have had more difficulty in finding a mate that meets their *high expectations*, given their own high level of achievement. This problem is magnified as the acceptable male population shrinks due to smaller graduation rates and the factor of career intimidation.

There is a declining population of high-achievement men that satisfy the elevated expectations of the successful woman.

How do women survive and thrive in the new world in which so much is expected of them and they expect so much of themselves?

For women who have been raised, almost relentlessly in some cases, to achieve, achieve, achieve, and be competitive with the world, it is difficult to suddenly tell yourself to defer to a man—your partner and lover. But try to keep this in mind: Encourage the man to be the man, and pretend that the man is a force in the relationship and has an opinion that counts.

According to a survey released in the *Journal of Family Issues*, women were more likely to get divorced when they earned 60% or more of the household income.

No Time for Sex Tonight, Henry—I'm Running for Governor

I have seen many people of both sexes who were raised in a very focused manner to achieve and succeed. Their training, preparation, and caring were no less deliberate or structured than that of a young Thoroughbred horse for the Kentucky Derby. For these people, every event is a challenge to overcome, a test to finish number one—whether it's work or running a 5K race on a Saturday morning, or even making the bed. Everything they do must be performed at a high level. That's all wonderful, but it puts pressure on a romantic relationship. If you are one of these people, and you live with another just like you, remember to leave your ego at the door when you come home at night. Change gears for your lover. We must learn to compromise.

> *Even though so many of us have been raised and motivated to get the A grades and make the Dean's list, we have to lower our expectations and be willing to compromise when it comes to relationships.*

Ironically, or perhaps not ironically, I find that many of the female baby boomers who reached success in the corporate or medical world are starting to run out of gas. And that's OK. They tell me, "I don't need to make the extra $100K this year. I plan to work only three days per week and do part-time consulting." Some female heavy-hitters change to a less stressful job, albeit one that pays less. I am beginning to hear this from baby-boomer men as well.

I also see the results of long-term dedication and countless work hours beginning to influence the career decisions of their adult children. These children have been raised in a family of super-achievers charging along in the career rat race, challenging themselves to make more money, get the promotion, buy the McMansion in the burbs, and drive the BMW SUV. Many of their children raised in this environment have experienced the collateral turmoil and neglect from this journey. It's not surprising that many of this young generation do not want to participate in the same kind of life plan.

Unconditional Love Sucks!

Yes, they will attend college, but instead of getting that job on Wall Street, many will opt to run a little ice cream shop on Main Street. I especially see this from children of upper middle class families.

- 60% of professional women under 30 aspire to be a CEO. After 30, only 37% have the same goal.
- Male-female entry jobs are currently 50-50. But men outnumber women by two to one for the next promotion.
- 25% of senior female executives are single. Only 10% of male execs are single.

(Source: LeanIN.org/McKinsey & Co. 2017 Report, *Women in the Workplace*)

In Alan Greenspan's book, *The Age of Turbulence,* he talks about measuring happiness. Findings show that upper income people have about the same degree of happiness as their lower income counterparts. Where the additional or less happiness occurs is when people are transitioning from one strata to another. Therefore, if you are going from poor to rich, you are happier during the transition. If you go from rich to poor, you are less happy—OK, miserable—but once you get to where you're going, there is not much happiness difference. What's the lesson? Happiness highs and lows are temporary. So do not do self-destructive things in your life if times are currently tough, including hanging around with losers just to feel better. Or hanging around with a jerky CEO because you'll think he'll bring you happiness later.

There's a financial lesson for all of us, too. I have already described the clients who make $400,000 per year, and they are always broke. Why can't the bigshot save any money? Lifestyle expectations are too high. Their standard of living, that is, their spending, goes up faster than their income. The $400,000 person may end up thinking they want or need to go out and buy a new showy car, a new house, more expensive clothes, and eat at fancier restaurants. You get the idea. I have known someone who makes almost a million dollars per year sit across the desk from me and tell me, with all sincerity and no hint of irony, "You wonder where it all goes."

How does this relate to the new roles of women and men? So often, I have seen couples who are over-achievers, on their quest to buy everything and do everything, go broke and get into an unmanageable level of debt. This leads to unmet expectations and mutual misery.

Jim, Darling, I'm Working Late Tonight with My Assistant, Max. Don't Wait Up.

The potential danger with many women and men in the work place has existed for many years. Spending lots of time provides opportunity for new and close relationships with the opposite sex. Because you work hard at the office and at home, there is a stronger inclination to feel under-appreciated at home, and may even feel, due to all your accomplishments, some entitlement to having social experiences on the outside your romantic partnership.

But be careful: There is a stronger likelihood of straying to adulterous affairs. If you want to preserve your current relationship, you will have to set very clear boundaries for yourself as to what you will and won't do with your colleagues. Once the boundary line is broken, you may never be able to return to your original spot.

If you respond to my exhortations with, "Well, I just enjoy hanging out with my workmates sometimes better than my bedmate," it means you already have a very tenuous relationship with your partner. Try to break it off now and move on instead of getting into the crazy game of multiple relationships.

Pre-define your boundaries with others in the workplace in order to save the relationship with your partner. For sure, social websites are a boundary to be recognized. Reports indicate anywhere between 10 and 20 percent of all affairs begin online. Most others start at work. If you find yourself being tempted by such boundaries, it is an obvious sign of relationship problems. Once a relationship is in trouble, the chance of future success with the person is doubtful. Relying on counseling to fix things afterwards is a dangerous strategy. As I said before, the cheated-on may tell themselves (and you) that they forgive, but they do not forget. I think my first spouse and I went to one, two, and maybe four counselors. The only result: Larger medical tax deductions.

Ladies, sure you can seek out that somebody who is more an achiever than you, but the results may disappoint. Let's say that you are a superstar female lawyer. And you tell yourself: "In order to find another superstar attorney mate, I am going to continue to look, even if it takes many years." Maybe you will find him, but perhaps you won't. If he is a superstar, you may be surprised to find yourself bumped down to be the second stringer in the family. You may not like this. The bottom line: Keep your mind open to different types of male partners. If you are a female doctor, you may be happier with a macho male plumber than with another doctor. Conversely, if you are a female general building contractor, it may not be a bad idea to be with an Amiable Jimmy Fallon type.

I find that of all my clients who have successful long-term relationships, one of the characteristics prevalent is an underlying mutual respect and even admiration for each other. One partner appreciates the talents or qualities in the other that perhaps they lack themselves. This may be difficult to attain if one dentist marries another dentist.

Look, Honey, Can You Do 50 Sit-ups Like Me?

One of the things I've noticed of couples is a new competitiveness between themselves. I think we have to be aware of this dangerous trend and be cautious of it getting out of hand. I especially see it when couples are participating in sports together, whether it's cycling, tennis, at the gym, or even playing ping pong in the garage. Females have been groomed, more than in the past, to be competitive in order to move onto and up the career ladder. I have observed this competitive inclination spill over to their love relationship. Be careful!

Yes, you can play tennis with your husband, but don't brag at the club how you whipped his ass a few hours ago. Or what's even worse: Telling him that after you have just a little more time and practice, you'll definitely be able to whip his ass. Give guys a break and tell them that they can play/ride/swing better than you, and that you are here playing tennis just because you like our company. As incredible as it seems as you read this, they will believe you.

A Happy Job Means a Happy Life

With regard to career choices, women may have more flexibility and opportunities in the community professions such as a doctor or lawyer, in which they can run their own office and set their own hours, and still have the wherewithal to have children. This is by no means a slight to women readers—just the opposite. Your multiple talents, goals and activities, both with the family and professionally, will constantly pull you in different directions to create stress.

Contrast working in your community with that of a large corporation, which may bring more rigid demands on schedule and deadlines and travel. In such an environment, there are also more office politics, causing more uncertainty regarding promotions and interpersonal relationships, including affairs. Working for a large entity also brings with it the possibility of a transfer to another location and the different way of life it may bring (e.g., a Philadelphia suburb versus downtown San Francisco). Of course, if you are a young over-achiever female coming out of college, and Microsoft comes along with that great offer, it will be difficult to refuse, but be aware of the long-term challenges.

People have complained that there are not enough women in top corporate positions yet. This trend is evolving and it can be done. Man or woman, realize that if you decide you want to start climbing that corporate ladder, it is more than full time—both physically and emotionally. It is a life commitment, 12 hours a day—or more if you're travelling with the job—and for many of us, including many men—not a desired life style.

Just Fedex Your Sperm Over and I'll Call You in the Morning—Maybe

It will be interesting to see in ten or fifteen years the trend of relationships between the sexes. How will the different roles fit in with each other? Will the professional woman feel fulfilled in her growing dominant role, and will the man feel that he is still contributing something important and necessary? Consider where we are going with the internet and artificial intelligence, which are changing basic communication methods. Yes, a text here and an email there allow us to communicate more frequently with each other in different formats, but it also allows us to stay in our own cocoon. Technology is making relationships more intimidating and, well, inconvenient. And even unnecessary. I know several people that feel much more comfortable with internet relationships behind the safety of their keyboard, rather than physically being with someone. This, hand in hand with the new role of women, will create troublesome effects for women *and* men. Do not be surprised if a future generation rebels against this current revolution of communication and even the roles of the sexes, and allows for more conventional paths that we have seen in the past. Trends cycle around, and male-female relationship roles may not be exempt from such a pattern.

In the 2017 science-fiction film, *Blade Runner 2049*, I found more interesting the writers' take on male-female relationships than the life-and-death battles portrayed. The main character, K, played by Ryan Gosling, is a bioengineered human and is conveniently human enough to have a sex drive. But instead of a regular partner—or God forbid, a wife—he has a beautiful holographic girlfriend named Luv who is there to satisfy his every need and desire. The holograph is the end-all of his romantic life. I thought it was interesting, however, that the movie failed to explore the companionship evolution of females. How were *their* needs satisfied in the year 2049? Would they ever need men in the future? When I asked my wife about this, her response was simple: Why would the screenwriters care about *that*? *They* were all men.

That Damn Darwin

As I talk about the challenges of the modern female and their effect on relationships, I have seen many experts, including women, suggest a solution: the househusband.

Unfortunately, we are left to deal with the realities of biology. At least for the time being, the biology of the sexes tells us that most women want to find someone to help protect them and their children. And men have naturally wanted to find someone to protect and shelter.

The Woody vs. The Rock Principle

I describe this natural male-female dynamic as the *Woody vs. The Rock* principle. Yes, that's right, filmmakers Woody Allen and Dwayne "The Rock" Johnson. Woody Allen, at least through many of his film characters, is the modern unmacho, insecure man, who muddles through life and desperately hopes that women will find him irresistibly cute and cuddly, and that they will protect and cling to him. In a scene from *Annie Hall,* when he is called in by Diane Keaton's character to kill a spider she found, he tells her, no problem, he's been killing spiders since the age of 30. It's a great joke because the character he portrays makes us believe there is probably a lot of truth to it.

Contrast this to The Rock. In most of his movies, he usually single-handedly saves the entire world. If The Rock had to recite the Woody Allen spider joke in a movie, the audience would not laugh; they'd be confused.

But we're not surprised when The Rock says to an opponent during one of his pre-Hollywood era wrestling matches, "Pull your pants down and prove that you are not a woman."

The Rock not only fights and defeats armies of bad guys, he usually gets the girl, too. This is not an accident. Contrast this to Annie, the title character in Annie Hall, who leaves Allen for an L.A. musician.

The male challenge: To possess traits of Woody AND The Rock

We men can not fool ourselves into thinking that women will stop looking for their Rock. All of us guys have to have some Rock in us. Women love the sense of being protected, the assurance that we will stand up and defend them. Defend them against the rude clerk in the store, the bully at the gas station, or the disparaging insurance agent. Throughout time, everyone has asked, "Why on earth do women like nasty men? What is the attraction?" And, in this day and age, because of the prevalent gentle man, it is almost counterintuitive to think that women would go for such a guy. But given human nature, or rather woman nature, it's no surprise. In fact, it's very basic.

Bad men, nasty men, are perceived to be leaders of the pack. Men who will be willing to protect and defend—even physically, if possible. Women are drawn to this trait in men.

And it doesn't matter that many of these same women are quite capable to confront difficult situations with their own assertiveness to resolve a problem. A female surgeon may end up marrying the Analytical accountant, but she still looks for him to possess some of The Rock kick-ass spirit. He may not have to defend his wife against wild animals, but he can sure help her at the auto repair shop, or tell the plumber that his overpriced invoice is bullshit. Most importantly, he must be there to defend the honor of his lady if she is publicly insulted or embarrassed.

It is not only important to possess some of The Rock spirit; your lover must be made aware it exists for her benefit.

Men are making a big mistake if they fail to realize, even in this day of metro-sexuality, that women like the guy who has some of The Rock in him. Corresponding tip to the men: You may *not* want to be the guy who is interested in what flower design the new couch has, or whether the bed sheets are folded correctly, or what the wording in the birthday card is. As much as women's roles have changed, it doesn't change what they look for in a man.

Guys, when we kiss our lady goodbye in the morning as they leave for their work, their briefcase in hand, be aware that they are working and meeting with potential Dwayne Johnsons out there—not just the wimpy Woody you met at the company picnic.

Fellows, if your partner is a high-powered female who has a child, has the good job, and a social life (sounds easier than it actually is, right, ladies?), she does not need you unconditionally. And if you are not bringing your best to the relationship, she may have little trouble finding somebody else. There are lots of people who could end up being your competitors at work or on your kids' soccer field. Never assume that the status quo will be the status quo forever. *When things fall apart, the partner who hasn't found a new lover mistakenly clings to the myth of unconditional love when desperately looking for answers.*

Waiter, It's His Check this Time

Let me give you an illustration how the traditional convention still exists—so far. I've asked friends and clients about what the woman expects from the man when they go out together at a restaurant on a first date—particularly in this era in which the woman often out-earns the man. For instance, who picks up the check? In this age of equality, one might think the high-income female would offer to pick up the check or at least split it. Perhaps on the first date.

Almost unanimously, older and younger females alike, responded that on the second date they expect the man to pick up the check. Why? What are they really saying? It's not because women are cheaper than men. It's not because they believe the man is taking advantage of them if the woman pays. It is because of this natural desire to be cared for and protected. And as barbaric as it may sound in this day- and-age, women still expect the man to bring home some bacon, even if it's in the form of whipping out a credit card at Longhorn Steakhouse.

For couples who have been in a long-term relationship together, who picks up the check? Does the expectation change? Some of the younger women told me there is some flexibility depending upon income, occasion, and perhaps who treated last time. They were not decisive in relying on a set rule. However, the older women were very decisive: "No, it doesn't change, the man should still pick up the check." And both generations of female respondents indicated that if the dinner out was with another couple, the man should be prepared to get the check, even if his wife has to refund him later (or he secretly has her credit card in his wallet). Call it an expectation of chivalry among the tribe.

This theme of expectation, carried throughout this entire book, is certainly reinforced here, even in our era of changing roles. The result of confused expectations places more pressure on relationships, more pressure on men to successfully maintain these relationships, and more pressure on women to find a man who meets her expectations, especially in light of her own accomplishments.

Make Sure There's Always a Little of The Rock

There are fewer and fewer areas where the man has their own domain. When I was a kid, most men worked on their cars or did some carpentry, so they could hang out in the garage or basement, put the radio on to their favorite station, and look at the calendar pinup girl on the wall. That era is pretty much gone. Who can work on their own car these days? Many of the formerly all-male social associations (Rotary, Kiwanis, golf clubs, etc.) have integrated women into their clubs. I think this could be detrimental to the male spirit, preventing him from having a little Rock time in his life.

In any relationship, the person who has the most earnings power usually has the most influence on the spending decisions and therefore the lifestyle of the couple. Generations ago, men decided how much car they could afford and how far away they could go on vacation. As the female becomes the dominant wage earner, her decision-making dominance and buying power will be felt, as advertisers already recognize.

Will this new dynamic of woman-power work for most men? I hear many males nonchalantly remark that if their wife wants to go out and kill themselves in the professional rat race, he is more than willing to stay home and cook dinner for the kids. But I do not believe such an attitude is sincere. Men in our society are doing things to offset their lesser masculine role. It is especially evident in a couple of areas. The almost overboard ritual of following American football on a Sunday afternoon is certainly one way for a guy to exert his masculinity, even if it is with pretzels in one hand and a beer in the other.

Another trend is the tendency, especially for the men we see in

Hollywood productions, to have a five o'clock—no, make that a midnight—shadow unshaved face, as if he has been living in the outback for the last several days hunting wild boar. This is an effort, of course, to make the man look more masculine. Ironically, when I talk to women about the unshaved look, they tell me it only looks good on a few men, that if we have gray whiskers it makes us look older, and finally, few women like to be kissed intimately by a man with a half-shaved, sandpaper face. So when the unshaved rugged-looking guy shows up in the new car TV commercial, he may look cool, but he's probably not getting any tonight.

Men, do not forget that if a potential mate is evaluating you and your unshaved look, they may wonder to themselves: "If he doesn't groom himself now, when he is obviously trying to impress a potential new lover, he'll probably look like a real slob after I commit to the guy." Oh, that's right—we have unconditional love that will override that concern: You can look like a slob later and she'll still love you? *Not* necessarily.

The changing role of women and men also reinforces the idea of separate checkbooks and separate assets. If a man has his own checkbook, he may maintain some of the financial power, if not as head of the family, then perhaps at least with himself. Additionally, recognizing the growing power of women in relationships, many women will just naturally want their own checkbook, which in my financial advisory experience has worked well.

Be careful, ladies, if your overpowering strength results in a debilitated man who lacks confidence with you. He may look elsewhere for the comfort of someone to nurture his manliness. Even if he is a house-dad with little extracurricular activities, the internet brings instant social access—and self-affirmation. It's so easy for people to find a chat room or social site to mingle with new friends. More than 20% of breakups are spurred by an online relationship. The internet, however, may be more the cause than the result of a failed relationship.

I'm not talking about sex when I say that women tend to want it both ways. Men do, too. Females want their own independence and the ability to make decisions that impact their lives, yet they still want a man who can show dominance when he needs to. At the same time, many of you guys are putting your feet up on the couch, fully aware that your honey is out working her ass off to bring the bacon home. Yet, as we relax, we often naively expect the respect that comes with a traditional male role. The juxtaposition of these two perspectives are likely to cause conflict.

Men, you will have to still earn your manly respect from your woman; but ladies, give him the opportunity to achieve your respect.

Part Three

PERSONALITY STYLES—SOME CONDITIONS ARE UNCONDITIONAL

Chapter 10
Predictable Behaviors You'll Be Stuck With

Sam: "No one will ever believe we were married sober."
—Movie, *Woman of the Year*, 1942

If romantic love is indeed conditional, what conditions of a relationship are we going to face?

It will depend, in large part, on the personality style of your partner.

As in the rest of the book, we have been describing factors that affect and predict the success of an intimate relationship. Let's admit to ourselves that it's a miracle any two people can live together for several years, putting up with each other's bad habits, and yes, constantly having to forget the pain inflicted on each other. We inflict pain, in part, because our partners are easy targets. You can bet that if I have a bad day at work, I am going to go home and take it out on my spouse. But why should she have to put up with that crap? And how long will she?

There are factors in my personality that are part of my package—call it the baggage I bring to the party. As much as I try to bring my best game to my relationship, my partner will be stuck with some of my personality baggage. For polite discussion, I call it personality style.

This chapter talks about personality styles and the four major quadrants or categories. You should know these, not only for your love relationships, but for all relationships, including friends, parents, bosses, customers, and coworkers. Once you know these personality types, you will know what to expect of the people you meet—and what they expect of you. I use it every day of my life and reference it with every person I meet, literally within two minutes of dealing with someone. Often, I can adjust my behavior—and expectations—to fit their style.

This concept is not my idea, nor is it new. I learned about these categories more than 30 years ago. What the experts have done is to separate personalities into four basic profiles, and by doing this, make it easier to sum up a person's predicted behavior and even how they view the world. These categories also predict how that person will react to another person's behavior. Much of the pioneering work in this area was done by David W. Merrill and Roger Reid. Reference: Reports on Personality Styles and Effective Performance (1981).

Just as most of us are not of one genetic trait, neither do we exhibit a pure personality style. We are a blend. But of these four categories that we're going to discuss, we can usually identify the dominant one that predominantly guides us through our everyday life. And in many cases, this dominant style guides us through major decisions.

The four types are:
1. Driver
2. Analytical
3. Expressive
4. Amiable

Over the years, I have heard these categories casually described with different terms, such as, extrovert and introvert, A-type and B-type. But I will show how the terms I prefer are the more descriptive—and more useful—for really knowing what to expect from another person.

To illustrate the shortcomings of over-simplified characterizations, consider this example: sex symbol Marilyn Monroe described herself as an introvert. But so has President George H.W. Bush (the elder) as well as Facebook founder Mark Zuckerberg. Would you expect similar relationship experiences with each?

Let's stick with celebrities for the moment—one dead, one alive. Both Robin Williams and Donald Trump would be considered extroverts. Would you, therefore, conclude that taking a two-week vacation with the late Robin Williams would be a similar adventure to one with the Trumpster?

You see, we need to more clearly—but still simply—define personality styles so that we can better predict what we face if we decide to have a fling with that engineer or marry the rich attorney. Knowing these profiles also allows us to keep our expectations in check. You'll come to understand your partner's limitations so that if you fall for a manufacturing foreman, you won't expect him to change into a Jimmy Fallon three years from now.

Styles shown in the quadrant above help us do just that.

Let's take a look at each profile, then we'll use them to do various love match-ups—and some love mix-ups.

THE DRIVER PERSONALITY STYLE: GET OUT OF MY WAY, I'M ON A MISSION

Famous Drivers: Hillary Clinton, George Washington, Richard Nixon, Donald Trump, Apple co-founder Steve Jobs, reality star Kris Jenner, entertainers Jennifer Lopez and Taylor Swift.

Are you a Driver? Just give it to me straight:
1. Very bottom-line oriented
2. Makes decisions quickly
3. Not the greatest bedside manner
4. Does not tell jokes—or tells them poorly
5. Would rather poison their dog than lay on a beach for vacation
6. Won't give a crap about reading all (or any?) of this book

People who are Drivers are very bottom-line, achievement, and success oriented. They don't care much about the *process* of doing something or about the experience of getting someplace; they just want to get there. They do not marvel at analyzing why someone or something else did what it did. They are usually not good at telling jokes and often are not even good at small talk. Saying that these people are "A" personalities is mostly true, but it's like the square and rectangle thing: Most Drivers are "A" personalities, but not all "A" personalities are Drivers. It's the same with classifying someone simply as an "extrovert." I'll explain.

Drivers Drive Us Crazy

Personality types cross political lines, and you'll discover that these personality quadrants cross financial and age lines, too.

When I meet a potential new client who wants to know exactly the investment results I can produce for them, and by what date, and they could care less about the detail, I am probably dealing with a Driver. When a Driver comes into my office, I don't have to worry about creating small talk, I don't have to worry about telling a joke. I also don't even worry about digging through files and fancy graphs for lots of detail and back-up. Drivers would quickly grow impatient.

When a Driver meets me, they work quickly to size me up, that is, to evaluate what ability I have to help them in their mission. They want to know the bottom line and what I can promise with investment returns. Legally, I am not allowed to offer any promise or commitment of return; this frustrates the hell out of them.

Within five minutes, they are either very happy with me or think I am useless.

When you are dealing with a Driver, be prepared to perform for results. If you do not help the Driver get to *their* desired bottom line, life will be hell for you. If you are in a relationship with someone who is a Driver, you will only be happy in the relationship if you, in turn, get satisfaction by helping him or her achieve their bottom line. If you fail to contribute to their mission, either because you care about your own mission or you are just ineffective, the relationship probably won't last. To keep them satisfied, you tow along or get dumped.

When you drive by the big houses in the fancy neighborhoods occupied by corporate executives or successful doctors, you say to yourself—and perhaps your mother wishes—that you could be married to that home's breadwinner, male or female, luxuriating in the life of the well-to-do. But be careful. The person who pays the bills in that house could make your life a living hell.

And as we'll see later, not all successful people have to be Drivers. Each category of the quadrant has successful people. Therefore, don't despair if you are not a Driver—you can still attain great success. And you do not have to marry a Driver to do it, either.

We Drive Them Crazy, Too

If you are reading this, and realize that you are probably a Driver, then many of your romantic relationships are going to drive you crazy—because most people are *not* Drivers. Most of us are not so focused on the bottom line, and as you Drivers deal with us, we can be a frustrating challenge for you. As a Driver, you may initially think that life can't get any sweeter than dating that gorgeous blonde or hunky lifeguard. Your first gaze at them across the beach creates very few expectations, except perhaps the obvious one. But after hooking up in a relationship, you will have inherent expectations, and do not try to fool yourself or me—you will. You're going to have high expectations that your mate will, must, and should help you achieve *your* goals. You begin to immediately think that your bottom line is now the bottom-line of the partnership. "Well, honey, we're married now and we want to save 20% of our income so we can buy the beach house." Or, "Honey, I expect you to make $30,000 per year so *we* can buy the house *we* need to have." Suddenly, your relationship has many traits similar to a business contract rather than a romance.

At this juncture, if you're a Driver, you're probably asking yourself, "Yeah, and what's your point?"

Secret Disclosed: The previous two paragraphs probably were not needed, and do you know why? Drivers don't read books! They don't have time for such details. They don't want or need to analyze all this nonsense. Even if they are given this book as a gift, they will allow it to collect dust on the shelf, or at most, flip through it and look for the printed headlines. (Do you really believe Donald Trump or Hillary Clinton even thoroughly *read* their own books, let alone wrote them? Who has time for that?)

My favorite Driver of all time is Thornton Melon. No, he is not a real person, but the character played by Rodney Dangerfield in the film comedy *Back to School*. This guy Melon is extremely bottom-line. He's very successful at his clothing business, but never had time to finish school (think Steve Jobs, Bill Gates, Mark Zuckerberg, all college drop-outs). So his teenage son convinces him, through a hard-fought negotiation, to attend college. Melon's approach to college does not center around hours of study and writing papers. He delegates out all that petty stuff. In the movie, he even gets the real Kurt Vonnegut, a famous writer, in a cameo appearance, to write a paper for him—you guessed it—analyzing the works of Kurt Vonnegut. An unknowing professor gives the paper a grade of C, and Melon, true to his Driver character, ends up firing the hapless author for ineffectiveness. Now that's bottom line.

Best Mate for a Driver

If you are a Driver who managed to accidentally flip to this page, and you are wondering what category of person is the best partner for you, it is probably an Amiable. To find out about Amiables, keep on reading.

And, if you're still reading, who is the worse partner for you? It's a toss-up. Both Expressives and Analyticals will drive you crazy. When dating, you may find an Expressive more fun and enjoyable to be with, but you probably wish they were more Analytical after you marry.

Should a Driver hook-up with another Driver? I have seen it work—sometimes. The trick for success to this combination: Each Driver's goals have to mesh almost perfectly. If goals are different, there will be an uncomfortable clashing, each going in different directions until the relation fizzles out, or more likely explodes.

I have a set of friends who have a successful marriage, and both are Drivers. They both love and live to develop real estate. I believe this shared mission is a key to the success of their long-term relationship. However, as I review my client and friend list, I can find no other successful Driver-Driver long-term relationships. What a shame, right, because if two driven people can combine all this focus, they would create an awesome power couple. Be realistic: If you're a Driver, you are fighting the odds if you think you can win on this long shot.

Celebrity Drivers We Love—and May Not

As noted, we've had several U.S. presidents who are Drivers, but just as many who were not. Note how each of these personality styles crosses political party lines. It's fun to talk about the personality quadrants of presidents, because, like celebrities, we know them so well. And when I refer to their characteristics, you'll be likely to respond, "Oh, yeah, that's right." George Washington, Harry Truman, Richard Nixon, and Donald Trump are all Divers.

Washington was a classic. All business, all bottom-line. He wore a military uniform attending the Continental Congress meeting—even before we had an army! His biography and accomplishments are legendary. As a colonist, he initially got upset with the Brits, not because of his lofty ideals, but because he thought they were cheating him on his import purchases. You see, the Brits were interfering with his mission. It was not until later, when he began rubbing shoulders with other founding fathers, that he really began to espouse idealistic democratic thinking. But when he did, again, he was on a mission to carry it out. His achievements established the structure and tone of our country that still exist today. Hell, it is said that when he retired to Mount Vernon, he was the first leader of a nation to ever voluntarily surrender political power. In the history of the world! (Yes, read the previous two sentences again—an amazing fact.) If that wasn't enough, he even personally oversaw the design of Washington D.C., with Frenchman Pierre L'Enfant, because, damn it, somebody had to do it.

Get-Er-Done: Is there any more bottom-line decision than by another president, Harry Truman, in deciding to drop the atomic bomb on Japan to end World War II? As for Nixon, can you imagine his attempting to tell a joke, something that Drivers typically fail at?

Ah, then we come to the Trumpster. If we thought Rodney Dangerfield's Thornton Melon, stuck in college, typified a misfit, watching Donald Trump take on the presidency was painful for many, and probably for the man himself. Have you ever built a skyscraper? Well, I have—at least as an advisor consultant. The process is a conglomeration of *bottom-lines*: getting the right materials, ensuring the proper design, coordinating all the subcontractors, and of course, the two really big bottom lines: completing the thing on time and within budget. Oh, and I forgot the other bottom line: the building must stay up!

Constructing a building is Donald Trump's world. Now, you immerse him in Washington politics. The people there do not even know how to spell *bottom line*. Congress hasn't approved an annual budget in years, let alone balanced one. And they take more vacations than the Housewives of Beverly Hills. If Donald thought he knew the art of the deal before, he ain't seen nothin' yet. His brusque behavior and braggadocio annoys the hell out of most of my friends, but not typically my friends who are Drivers. Like Trump, they believe it sometimes takes a blunt instrument to get the job done in this world of red tape and dodgy characters.

As you read this, your once idealistic view of living in the ritzy suburbs with a wealthy spouse may be tempered by knowing you could get stuck with a Thornton Mellon—or Donald Trump. You have to ask yourself if driving that new Tesla is worth this kind of partner.

Which of these Drivers would you marry?

Show Me the Money

Have I said that Drivers are always financially successful? Well, I won't. Just because they are on a mission, it does not mean it is the correct, or most profitable, mission. Most Drivers also have poor personality skills, which can be their most critical detriment. I know other professional advisors who are more clever than I and more ambitious, but their income doesn't show it. Why? They don't usually read people well, and, if they are a Driver, they often run over their own clients, to the point of scaring them away. Their attitude of "Do it my way or the highway" frequently does not have a very good success rate.

Typical professions in which Drivers predominate: CEOs, construction people, and manufacturing managers.

Corporate leaders may be an obvious one, and I just described Trump in the construction industry. When you build, say, computers, you must be on a very focused mission to get the job done.

Unconditional Love Sucks!

Achieving time schedules, working within budget, and meeting specification requirements, all propel the manufacturing person.

And, even though you may want your manufacturer or builder to be a Driver, you probably would not want your designer or architect to be a Driver. If she is, you will probably end up firing her—if she doesn't fire you first.

My first finance job out of college was working in a Fortune 500 computer company's engineering and manufacturing division. The production mission was very focused, and the expected results were very real: if the computerized air traffic control system we built did not work, planes would crash. It didn't matter how charismatic the operations VP was, or how good he or she looked, or how well they wrote their reports. If the damn system didn't work at the end of the production line, we were in trouble.

Contrast this results-oriented process to the process of my next job: a consultant in New York City. It was a culture shock to me because our products were about charismatic persuasion, smooth personalities and fancy reports. There were far fewer Drivers in this environment.

Let's do a quick exercise. Fill in the blank.

Three Driver personalities you know:

_____

_____

_____

Now think: Hypothetically, could you stand to be married to them? And, if you have/had a child, do you want your child to be raised by one? Would you be happy if your child were married to one?

THE BOTTOM LINE FOR LOVERS WHO ARE DRIVERS

Their Plusses:

1. You know where they stand
2. Often hard worker
3. Very organized
4. Protective of their friends
5. Potential for high income
6. If they call you for a second date, they'll probably eventually propose

Their Minuses

1. It's their way or the highway
2. Not very introspective
3. Expect action—and reaction—before analysis
4. Not poetic
5. If you do not support their mission, it's good-bye

THE ANALYTICAL PERSONALITY STYLE: LET ME THINK ABOUT THAT

Famous Analyticals: President Jimmy Carter, Albert Einstein, Apple co-founder Steve Wozniak, comedian Jerry Seinfeld

Are you an Analytical? Analyze this:

1. You actually read instruction manuals
2. You can estimate how many slices of pizza are consumed annually in the U.S. (an actual Google job interview question)
3. Your room is the neatest in the house
4. You love planning the cross-country road trip—down to the Starbucks stops
5. You fear Donald Trump's rashness and you do not trust Hillary Clinton's scheming

Unconditional Love Sucks!

Analytical type personalities. We all know these people. They are the ones who love data, who love to tinker with all of the features of their new cell phone, and who have probably even read the fine print of the instruction manual. Give them a dull, small-print insurance policy, and they'll read every word. And they can drive us crazy with their need for more—and more—information before they can make a decision.

Salespeople hate Analyticals. Just when the salesperson thinks they have provided enough information to close the deal, the Analytical looks across the table and asks, with all sincerity, "Can you send me a little more information on this? I want to review this on the website and think about it a little longer." Salesperson to herself: "Get me the hell out of here!"

The Analytical is so busy reviewing and weighing and researching and evaluating that they often never come to a decision.

When an Analytical client comes into my office, I know to provide tons of information for that meeting. Even then, they may delay in a decision, and if they do decide to do something, often there is an external stimulus, like a deadline or another family member's influence—or impatience—that propels them to action.

They love detail. I show my Analytical clients all kinds of charts, historical data, financial statements. I give them reports that they can dwell on. And dwell on. And dwell on.

Analyticals are also the people who, when they buy a gadget or car, love to explain all of the excruciating features and components to their friends. Only they have discovered that if you click the hidden button under the steering wheel to the left twice, it will turn on the TV at home. Finally, their friend, exasperated or bored—unless she is also an Analytical—walks away or cries out, "Enough already!"

Some of the favorable characteristics of an Analytical: they're usually pretty level-headed and emotionally stable, they usually make a pretty good living, their tempers are pretty controlled, they are often very loyal and often very ethical. Why ethical? They love following rules. And if you don't follow rules, uncertainty thrives, which they cannot tolerate.

> *How do you drive an Analytical crazy? Fold a paper road map the wrong way while she watches. (That joke has become obsolete with Google maps.)*

Funny Thing About Analyticals

Analyticals are also neat. So, if you're a slob, you will have trouble with an Analytical. And, I don't have to tell the Analyticals who are reading this that you may have great frustration with slobs. What really frustrates the slobs is, just as Analyticals always need more and more information, they also need the room or office to be ever *more* neat. So, even after the slob relents by cleaning off the week-old popcorn from the coffee table, the Analytical will respond with, "Yes, but the magazines you left behind are not stacked perfectly straight."

Anaylticals may not be the most beautiful people, not because of a genetic defect, but just because flashy looks are not a priority with them, even though neatness is. Watch an old Seinfeld show. Jerry was not the least bit showy in appearance, but his clothes were remarkably, unnoticeably, very neat: perfectly ironed, appropriately buttoned, and no shirt tail ever dangling. If an Analytical has a hair style, get used to it, because they will probably never alter it. Has Jerry's hair ever changed?

You see, even comedians can be Analyticals.

I know few engineers, accountants, math teachers, or doctors who tell jokes well or at all. Jerry Seinfeld, whom I have referenced as an Analytical, tells jokes, and obviously very well, but much differently than, say, the late Robin Williams, a pure Expressive. Imagine those two on stage together—it would have been like oil and water. On the Seinfeld TV comedy series, Jerry's neighbor Kramer was a wonderful Expressive, and when they were in a scene together, Jerry would normally play the straight man to Kramer's craziness. In many scenes, one can actually observe Seinfeld (the man, not his character) struggling to hold in a laugh as Kramer goes through his wild antics.

We also see the analytical side of Jerry, not only in his clothes, but also in his jokes. His routines—hell, even his sitcom—dwell on evaluating various situations and then trying to figure them out.

Did the stand-up routines of Robin Williams or Rodney Dangerfield, real-life Expressives, ever get very analytical? No way, Jose'.

Rodney Dangerfield as his *Expressive* self: "When my wife asks me to take out the garbage, I tell her, 'why should I, *you* cooked it.'"

> Two famous comedians, Seinfeld and Dangerfield, both entertainers and apparent extroverts, are very different personality styles. To get along with Jerry, his wife will have to behave differently than if she was married to Rodney. Think about this when evaluating lovers. And don't fall for the "extrovert" classification myth.

If you are an Analytical planning a vacation, ask your partner what type of vacation he or she wants. If they leave it to you, you will doubtless review endless destination websites, compare prices, and evaluate options for the next three months before you finally decide how to do a simple trip. Even then, it will probably be the most detailed itinerary ever created.

Advice to Analyticals: Leave a free moment for a "spontaneous" walk on the beach. If your spouse, who may not be an Analytical, suggests getting off the trail to do an activity on the spur of the moment, play along. Please try, as much as it pains you. In fact, look forward to your partner's impulsiveness, because you don't have much yourself.

But that brings us to another wonderful trait of Analyticals: You are great planners for the future. My Analyticals are my best savers. They have the biggest 401K balances, and they always know how long they're going to keep a car before trading it in. And yes, they usually get an updated version of the same model.

Realize, if you are an Analytical, even on first impressions, you are not going to come across as the life of the party. And think what your spouse or partner will think of your excitement factor—ten years—ten long years—into the relationship. It could be very b-o-r-i-n-g for them. Consider this to be a challenge for you.

Honey, I've Calculated that We've Made Love 823.5 Times

How are Analyticals at romance? Not always so hot. If you see yourself fitting this mode, try to lighten up and not be so technical in your conversations. Try to be a little more fun for your partner and try not to dog him or her with a constant stream of information. Your new girlfriend probably does *not* want to see the 953 photos you took on your trip to Disney World last year, even if it was with your new Canon XP-453 camera with the new JZF super lens. (And, before you Analyticals research this particular camera, let me tell you that it really does not exist: I made it up!)

If you're an Analytical, which are the best personality types to date and be with? Your first impulse, believe it or not, will be to date someone who is *not* an analytical, because Analyticals may even bore *you*.

If you are dating an Analytical, resign yourself to accept that Analyticals may not be as outwardly affectionate or emotional as other personality categories. Don't be offended—it's not your fault. They may still love you to death—or to boredom—and be very loyal. And, as with other personality types, DO NOT EXPECT TO CHANGE THEM.

I know of a couple that dated and both were Analyticals. They had difficulty deciding whether to marry or not. They had trouble deciding whether to have children or not. After they finally married, they drove each other crazy with decision-making, especially when one of the two started a small business. When in business for yourself, decisive action is necessary. It is no coincidence that the words decisive and decision share the same root. In business for yourself, at some point, often sooner rather than later, you have to stop weighing options and act on an issue and then move on the issue. Otherwise, it is anguish for everyone affected.

After the partner started the enterprise and discovered she needed help with decision-making, she recruited, guess-who, her mate to come into the business. Big mistake. So now, we had a new fledgling business with *two* Analyticals trying to analyze the business to success. Which vehicles are best, what advertising should be done, what prices should be charged, etc., etc. In a business—any business—the decisions are never ending.

Unconditional Love Sucks!

By now, you can understand that the stress between the two of them became unbearable. For them, it was fighting mother nature—their nature. Sadly, this terrible situation eventually broke up the business and their marriage.

You Drive Me Nuts!

A Driver, on the other hand, may drive the Analytical nuts because Drivers like to make decisions quickly. Having said that, this combination is often very successful, but often in terms of almost a business arrangement. The Analytical fills in the planning blanks for the Driver, while the Driver facilitates accomplishing tasks that would otherwise paralyze the Analytical. Most Analyticals I know, especially those who are Republicans, loathe President Trump.

The best example of a well-known Driver-Analytical "marriage" is the business partnership of Steve Jobs (Driver) and Steve Wozniak (Analytical). The contribution of each made Apple possible, and without either one of them, there would be no company. However, their complicated relationship ended in a type of nasty divorce, primarily for classic reasons related to how each of these personality types sees the world. For a time, a third party, investor Mike Markkula, Jr., served as a referee and mediator, but even he could not hold them together.

What'd Ya Expect?—He's a Nuclear Engineer!

One president, Dwight D. Eisenhower, an Analytical, was a general during World War II. He methodically figured out how to organize all the allied forces to defeat Hitler, and that was before the aid of iPhones. But the classic presidential Analytical in recent generations was Jimmy Carter. His desk was always piled high with reports and data that he would review and analyze to death. Although his honesty and humility is what the nation dearly needed after the Nixon era, Carter often had difficulty making the big decision and was not very effective at delegating. We should not be surprised because, after all, he was a trained nuclear engineer. If you meet an engineer, there is a high probability that he or she is an Analytical.

While we are talking about the professions of typical Analyticals, don't forget to include accountants, scientists, software and computer engineers, doctors, and many teachers. So, if you are about to connect with a person in one of these areas, be prepared for lots of data and someone who will probably not be the life of the party. And remember to keep your shirt tucked in.

Fill in the blank. Three Analytical personalities you know:

_____
_____
_____

Now think: Hypothetically, could you stand to be married to them? And, if you have/had a child, would you be happy if your child were married to them?

ANALYTICAL PARTNERS: THE FINAL ANALYSIS

Their Plusses
1. They are thoughtful: analysis before action
2. Good, steady wealth builders
3. Decent conversationalists
4. Usually even-tempered
5. Often above-average income
6. Quiet and reserved in manner
7. They do all the planning, while you go along for the ride

Their Minuses
1. Analysis paralysis with decision-making at times
2. Lack of spontaneity
3. Tedious
4. Often judgmental
6. Unexciting on dates

THE EXPRESSIVE PERSONALITY STYLE: SO THREE GUYS WALK INTO A BAR...

Famous Expressives: Presidents Bill Clinton and John Kennedy, Britney Spears, actress Marylin Monroe, businessman billionaire Mark Cuban

Unconditional Love Sucks!

Are you an Expressive? Expressly so if:
1. The last thing you *planned in advance* was deciding how many six packs to take on your boat.
2. You love to tell jokes, and you're good at it—at least *you* think so.
3. You may be the life of the party, but may not be invited back after you get accused of flirting with the host's partner.
4. People wrongly accuse you of having a temper, even *after* you fix the wall you put your fist through.
5. Your most frequent expression to your lover, right after "I love you," is, "I'm sorry I was such an ass."

Without Expressives, the world would survive, but it wouldn't have nearly as much fun. They don't just bring life to a party, they *are* the party. We can easily point out Expressives because they are the most fun to be with at a gathering, on a trip, at a dinner. They like to sit at the bar to have a drink, and after 30 minutes will know the bartender's entire life story. But the bartender is going to know *thei*r life story in 15 minutes. These are the people who sit next to you on the airplane and want to talk. They typically land in careers as the jovial sales person or the (overly) dramatic actor. When you greet them, they will have the joke of the day for you.

Studies have shown that approximately 50% of our population falls into this category. Now you know why bars and nightclubs are filled on Friday nights. And why parking lots are filled before football games with tailgaters.

Unfortunately, the other side of the Expressive is not as amusing: living by impulse, poor planners, not exactly the most loyal people, more adulterous than the other categories, and even though they have the loudest laugh in the room at the party, they also have the hottest temper. When an Expressive turns mean, look out.

Still, with all these cautionary characteristics, the other 50% of us are constantly falling for them. Expressives are a great time on a date, especially if you have expectations that do not extend beyond having a fun evening.

Looks Can Be Deceiving

I have seen Expressives that are very neat, and others that are slobs, and even some who go back and forth in this area. Accordingly, don't be fooled if they happen to iron their pants for a date.

If you are *with* an Expressive, you have to be prepared for impulse and spur of the moment stuff. If you don't like this type of behavior, you will end up on prescription medication for most of the relationship. If you like to plan things, if you like set routines, if you like showing up on time, Expressives will drive you bananas, because they often noticeably lack in these areas. Perhaps their charisma can overcome these deficiencies. If you can tolerate the weaknesses, God bless you.

On the other hand, if you *are* an Expressive, you probably don't even realize how you irritate people. And if you have other offsetting qualities, such as looks or athletic skills, or you're a successful salesperson, you may think you have the right to irritate people and that you are entitled to your behavior. And to a great extent, you may be. Ugh.

What are some of the professions where you'll commonly find Expressives? I have often found them in the teaching professions, not because they like math or social studies, but because they like the captive audience. As expected, then, entertainers are often in this category of personality style.

Sales people often fall into this category, but they are not always the *top* sales people. Why? Because they get distracted too easily. However, if you have a Driver who also has some Expressive characteristics, look out. They will be the best sales person in the company.

Many successful corporate executives have Expressive characteristics. Mark Cuban, billionaire owner of the NBA Mavericks and *Shark Tank* co-host, is a good example. In the course of his career, his list of activities illustrates this: During college, which he picked sight-unseen (adversity to planning), he taught disco dancing and did party planning (literally the life of the party). Later he became a software salesman, then got fired because he impulsively acted in his own interest with a customer. And of course, he was never happy to be just a rich, reclusive techy sports owner. He had to have his own TV show, too.

Another Expressive CEO is Richard Branson. He started Virgin records from a church building, and later started Virgin Airlines because he had a flight canceled while in Puerto Rico, having to charter his own flight. His head master at school declared that Branson would either become a millionaire—or end up in prison.

The Bill and Hillary Show

Expressive presidents include Bill Clinton. Nobody can tell a story better than Bill. Nobody has more charisma, and few can talk a better talk. Let's face it, who better could you spend an evening in a bar with than Bill—even if you're a Republican. Just ask the Bushes.

Even among Expressive *presidents*, you can see some adulterous characteristics. With all the problems Richard "I'm-no-crook" Nixon had, you don't hear much about his cheating on poor Pat. On the other hand, we generally idolize Kennedy by naming airports and boulevards after him, but he practically ran a whore house in the white house for young lady staffers who were barely of legal age.

We are talking about predictable traits here. Remember this: The theme is predictability. And when you meet an Expressive, you'll tell yourself, "I realize that I read that stupid book, but this person I am falling in love with is better than the typical Expressive, and, I can change this person so that he/she does not have the negatives that come with the positives. I really think this person is different." You are wrong today, and you'll be wrong tomorrow.

Personality styles do not change, or at least you cannot count on people changing. Get that through your romantic hopeful head. As explained earlier, we see just the opposite in movies all the time. While dating, the protagonist may be mean spirited, selfish, and obstinate, but then they fall in love with the co-star. And what does the co-star do? He or she assumes that after the honeymoon, the same mean-spirited person will not revert to the jerk. The movie ends, and we leave the theatre with a happily-ever-after glow. Thank God we don't have to hang around for the sequel that happens in real life.

An interesting analysis with Expressives is to look at the relationship between the Clintons, Bill and Hillary. Hillary, a Driver, has been married to Bill for more than 46 years. We know that Bill's behavior has understandably driven Hillary bonkers during much of this time. But we also know that Hillary, as a Driver, is interested in the bottom line and getting results, almost at any cost. The result: she puts up with Bill's antics because, despite his flaws, he helps her accomplish her mission, which is essentially achieving political power and wealth. If he lost elections, or was unsuccessful at his impeachment battle, or certainly if he were not the darling the of democratic party, it would be interesting to see if their marriage would still be intact.

On the other hand, after all these years, why hasn't Bill left Hillary for one of those women he has been with? The answer: He, like most Expressives, loves having a partner like Hillary who can accommodate and smooth the way for his behavior. Her abilities to help plan, focus, and get Bill to the finish line are indispensable to her husband's success. He knows all this better than anyone, and as a result, I believe Bill has respect, and even true love for his wife. Notwithstanding his affection, however, he still cannot change his Expressive ways, nor should Hillary ever expect him to.

Ah, you ask, but how much does Hillary love *Bill* after all the apparent heartache he has put her through? I don't know, and maybe she doesn't, but probably she does. As I have asserted earlier about Drivers, they tend to evaluate relationships and activities more on the results than on the process, and overall, the Clintons have had, and continue to have, an amazing run. Hillary takes stock of that and values Bill's role in their accomplishments, and for this reason, will continue to stay with him and value their relationship.

How would you feel if you were in Hillary's place? It depends, in part, what your personality type is.

An Analytical would forgive Bill for the first or even second scandal, having weighed the advantages and disadvantages of leaving. But, after the second misstep, the Analytical would probably re-evaluate the situation, analyze whether they could shame their partner, and if they believed the odds were slim, would end up walking out.

How Lucky Do You Feel, Punk?

I'm not the first person to think that the relationship between the Clintons is quite fascinating. It becomes clearer though when viewed through the prism of personality types. We talk about these personality classifications and I think it makes it even more interesting with how this particular couple survives in their relationship. It's also interesting to note that Bill has not cheated on Hillary just once or twice. He's done it several times and even more times than we may know. But yet, Hillary has stayed with him. And, Hillary has not been able to change him. You would think the embarrassment of public scorn, or the shame of husbandly guilt would stop him doing what he has done, but it has not. He's done it over and over again. Perhaps only the aging process will slow him down. This is a lesson for those of us who are dealing with Expressives.

If you are reading this, and you know by now that you are an Expressive personality, you have to ask yourself, as Clint Eastwood's Dirty Harry would ask, "How lucky do you feel, punk?" How much can you get away with? Unfortunately—or perhaps fortunately for you—your partner may be very lenient with you, too. Ironically, Hillary, a strong Driver, is so focused on her bottom line that she ends up being extremely lenient with her husband, even though we may initially think that such a strong woman would put her foot down—or up his ass—to kick him the hell out. But as of this writing, she has not.

Does Bill realize all of this? Absolutely. And with his abilities, he probably does instinctively. Does he know his boundaries? Do they have an explicit agreement between them for what those boundaries might be? I don't know. I do believe, however, that his boundaries for indiscretions have recently shrunk since his wife lost what probably will be her final run for the presidency. This may also appear to be an irony. Now that Hillary is not seeking the presidency, she doesn't need Bill as much, and he therefore has lost his leverage in the relationship.

Expressives Get Around

So, as you Expressives out there mull over your own leverage, think about what is in it for your spouse or partner to put up with your personality style.

As we look at relationships that an Expressive personality may have, probably the most explosive is with another Expressive. From a distance, it's easy to understand why. We have two impulsive people, who do not plan well, who manage their lives through emotion, who both need to be center stage, and who will have problems staying monogamous. What if Bill were married to another Expressive? Between the two of them, there would probably have been so much chaos, the marriage would have quickly spun out of control, like a plane nosediving to the ground.

A formula for disaster, right? So, we never see it, right? Wrong. We see it all the time, and most visibly with Hollywood celebrities, who boast a large stable of Expressives. Should we really be surprised when we hear that Nicholas Cage has been married five times? Or Kim Kardashian, has had three weddings? For the trivia readers, you'll know that the late Zsa Zsa Gabor beats them both with nine walks down the aisle. I give credit to Brad Pitt and Angelina Jolie making their marriage work for as long as they did. Angelina has been married three times.

Strangely enough, several famous comedians, whom one would think are the quintessential Expressives, have had very long marriages. I don't say that they are perfect marriages, but Bob Hope was married more than 60 years; Don Rickles, 52 years; and yes, even Bill Cosby has been married 59 years. Remember, I said they weren't always perfect. Jerry Seinfeld, starting late in life, has been wed 22 years. You already know the key to Jerry's success—he's not actually an Expressive. The key to the success of other comedians, especially ones who are Expressives: they did not marry other Expressives.

I feel bad for celebrities who have Expressive personalities. It is probably difficult for them to hook-up with interesting people outside of their celebrity bubble, which is loaded with other Expressives. We talked earlier about the problems that Leonardo DiCaprio has on the dating scene. Non-celebrities cannot understand the pressures of the show business industry and its constraints, so it's probably very natural for a person in that rich and famous world to be attracted to someone similar to themselves. Plus, let's face it, there are lots of really great-looking people in this bubble. Add to these circumstances the fact that their "office" is the set of a movie or TV show, where they are working and bonding with co-workers, no different than a computer programmer bonding with another programmer at a place like Google. Celebrities, however, don't have the opportunity or inclination to look for dates on eHarmony.

Unconditional Love Sucks!

Expressives are naturals at new relationships. They are great at parties, they thrive when there are few expectations, and their impulsive behavior is so much fun. You'll never have more excitement than dating an Expressive—at least in the beginning. That's why so many of us fall in love with Expressives, only later to ask ourselves, how the hell could I have done that?

I think that if more of the people in Hollywood were able to meet other non-Expressive types, they would have more successful marriages, although the thrill of new love may not be as much fun. Unfortunately, the people who are *not* celebrities are also not likely to be as physically attractive or carry the status an A-lister believes they need.

Alec Baldwin and Kim Basinger, two Expressives, had a famously volatile marriage. And then there is Charlie Sheen who takes volatile to a new level.

How do Expressives get along with Analyticals? Pretty well, especially in the short term. Expressives like having Analyticals around because they can do the planning for their impulsive, live-for-today mate. Analyticals keep life organized while the Expressive is entertaining the world and themselves. Normally, in the short run, Analyticals love being around Expressives, especially if they don't have to depend on them. At the beginning of a relationship, say at a party, it is very comfortable for the Analytical to sit back and be amused by the Expressive.

The problems occur in longer term relationships. The Analytical, at the end of the day, loves their life organized and predictable. Then, life is thrown into chaos—at least from their point of view—by the Expressive. So, if you are an Expressive, try to marry an Analytical, but keep yourself under control so you don't drive them totally crazy. They'll keep your life running smoothly.

A famous Expressive-Analytical couple from many years ago was iconic actress Marilyn Monroe and third husband Arthur Miller. By now you can understand that Marilyn is the classic Expressive, living life emotionally and impulsively, but lost in drugs, and hearing voices in her mind that we can never understand. Miller, on the other hand, was one of the great American playwrights of the 20th century. His plays were meticulously crafted and deep analytical studies of the American dream and its nightmares. When the sex symbol came into his life, she was the American dream and nightmare all wrapped up in one tempting package. Miller, upon falling in love with her, thought he could analyze Marilyn, figure her out, then change her, as if he were revising a draft of a play. But he never could.

This is how Miller put it in his later years, talking about Marilyn as seen in a 2017 HBO documentary produced by daughter Rebecca Miller: "People were far more difficult to change than I'd ever realize." They divorced one year before her death.

My advice to Analyticals attached to an Expressive: Date the Expressive, but don't marry them.

We have not talked about Expressives matched up with the Amiable personality profile. Like Analyticals, Amiables are so often enamored with the charismatic and fun Expressive, they either put up with him or her, or believe their lover will change, either with help or with the passing of time. If you are one of these people who want to have patience with your Expressive, be prepared for lots of work and frustration.

At the end of the day, the best choice for the Expressive, and maybe all of us, is to hook up with an Amiable, whom we discuss next.

Fill in the blank. Three Expressive personalities you know:

_____
_____
_____

Now think: Hypothetically, could you stand to be married to them? And, if you have/had a child, would you be happy if your child were married to them?

THE GOOD, BAD, AND BEAUTIFUL OF EXPRESSIVE PARTNERS SUMMED UP

Their Plusses:
1. Enjoyable first dates
2. Charismatic
3. Spontaneously fun
4. Very touchy feely—"I feel your pain."

5. Adept at adapting to others' personalities in order to be more relatable
6. Potential for good income
7. They love the thrill of a new love

Their Minuses

1. Poor planners
2. Action and words before thinking through
3. Overly emotional/sensitive
4. Susceptible to impulse
5. Hot tempered—but doesn't stay mad long
6. Potential for being broke a year after making lots of money
7. They love the thrill of a new love (Yes, a minus, too)

THE AMIABLE PERSONALITY STYLE:
SOUNDS GOOD TO ME!

Famous Amiables: Both presidents Bush, Prince Harry, Jimmy Fallon, maybe Nicole Kidman.

Are you an Amiable? You'll probably agree you are if:

1. Your partner will decide which TV show the two of you watch tonight, and you'll go along to get along.
2. Embarrassment is almost as painful as death itself—no, it's worse.
3. A lover has inflicted abuse (through adultery, addiction, or physically), and the lover remained your partner.
4. Self-motivation is often in doubt.
5. You're reading this book as a favor to someone else.

Take a Vacation with an Amiable

Amiables are generally people who go along with the crowd and want to please others. If you ask them what they would like to do tonight, they'll turn around and ask what *you* would like to do. If you're going out to dinner, and you ask them where they want to eat, they'll ask where do *you* want to eat. If you tell them you feel like Mexican food tonight, they'll say, that sounds good, let's do Mexican—even if they'd rather do Chinese:

"Do you want to eat Mexican tonight?

Amiable: "That's fine."

"Or would you prefer Italian?"

Amiable: "That's OK, too."

"How about eating last week's left-overs out of the garbage?"

Amiable: "No problem—give me a minute to get some silverware."

Amiables are most concerned with keeping others happy. They are afraid of being out of step with others, including a group of friends, their loved ones, and people at work. For sure, they're usually great to supervise at the office because they don't give you a song and dance when you ask them to do something. And, they are usually great friends because they do not cause a stir when planning activities.

Amiables like people, but because they are nervous about screwing up something, they often are hesitant to invite people to their homes or suggest a social gathering. Other people often take this as aloofness or even rudeness, but it is not.

Amiables make terrible sales people because there is no way that they want to hear rejection. They do not want to impose on another's will. For instance, if a good insurance sales person is told by a prospect that they intend to live forever, the seller's response will be to site examples of premature deaths, often relating these events with drama and foreboding. If an Amiable sales person gets hit with the same rejection, they'll be afraid to disagree, even though they know the person just made an idiotic statement about living forever. It's just not in their nature.

Unlike Expressives and Drivers, Amiables usually have a low temper and a long fuse before they blow-up. You really have to push them to get them visibly aggravated. I said visibly because they are not numb—they may be burning inside, but they resist expressing it. They do not want to upset the status quo even though their likes and dislikes may be even stronger than yours. They will normally keep these opinions to themselves.

Even more rare is an Amiable who tells a joke. I have been with my wife, an Amiable, for 17 years, and have yet to hear her tell a joke. Not even a "Take my husband—please." Amiables always respond to our request for a joke with, "Oh, I can never remember jokes." Yes, Amiable talk-show hosts are the exception.

One other thing about Amiables: they're great to confide in and share secrets and even gossip. People feel comfortable opening up to an Amiable. There is an implied trust, perhaps because the person confiding believes he or she will not be judged harshly by an Amiable.

For those of you who may be thinking about a relationship with an Amiable you've got your eye on, and at first glance you think they are shy, boring and unassuming, watch out. Amiables may not have confidence in many areas, but they make up for it in other ways. They are often great cooks—in the kitchen *and* bedroom, and lovely to travel with, because they are so easy to get along with. Have you ever tried travelling with a Driver? Oh my god, it's not easy. A common mistake for young people dating is to underestimate—or even ignore—the Amiable.

Even a go-along Amiable can be very successful in a career. Both Presidents Bush 41 and 43 have a dominant Amiable profile. George W, the younger, is generally easy going and hard to get angry. His desire to please friends is evidenced by his habit of developing endearing nicknames for those around him. Can you imagine Nixon doing this? Or Hillary? Many mistook this amiable trait of Bush for a country bumpkin mentality. But don't forget, he was smart enough to graduate from Yale and Harvard Business School, and by the way, win not one, but two terms as president of the United States—something that a smooth-talking genius like Mitt Romney could not do once. However, by the end of his administration, Bush's wife, Laura, a librarian by profession, had to become one of his major spokespersons to defend him, primarily because Amiables are not the most assertive communicators, either.

As you can see, the person holding the most powerful office in the world can be an Amiable. Not convinced yet? From recent history, President Gerald Ford was also an Amiable. It's interesting to note that both Bush and Ford had a reputation for physical clumsiness, often characteristic of Amiables. (Try Youtubing Ford tripping up and down steps.) This reputation persisted despite the fact that Ford was an All-American football player and captain of the team at the University of Michigan. Playing center *and* linebacker, he took the team to two undefeated seasons and national titles in 1932 and 1933. Meanwhile, George Bush, as of this writing, can out-bike 99% of the population. These reputations for being clumsy perhaps stem from their bending over backwards—almost literally—to be part of the crowd and *not* stand out.

Amiables tend to do some silly, embarrassing things. I think inherently the rest of us know that they are trying to be part of the group, to fit in. So, when something that they do is viewed as goofy, we pounce on them for it—because we know we can.

President Ford: There he goes again.

Amiables have wonderful powers of observation, however. They notice things and people and moods that most of us don't. Why? Because they are subconsciously afraid that if they are not on top of what's around them, they could be caught embarrassingly on the wrong step. So, an Amiable woman will notice details of what other women at a restaurant are wearing, and another Amiable will remember what drink his friend had at an earlier party.

Wake Me When You're Done

Amiables sound great to be with, right? What's their biggest sin? They can be viewed as boring personalities. Can you already see this in Bush and Ford? They don't tell jokes or dance on the table wearing a lamp shade at parties as Expressives do, and they hardly ever say mean things about neighbors that you would hear from Drivers. Like Amiables, Analyticals can be boring, too, but—and you can understand this after reading about them earlier—it's a different kind of boring. Analyticals bore you with *their* facts-and-figures point of view; Amiables bore you because they may not actively respond to *your* point-of-view. Yes, it's all about us.

And like Analyticals, Amiables have lots of wonderful knowledge and interesting perspectives, but notice, for instance, that they don't make the best guests on talk shows. Who can remember what Bush ever said on Jay Leno's Tonight Show? But those of us old enough can easily remember Bill Clinton playing his saxophone on a talk show. Who cares whether he was any good or not—it was fun to watch. Perhaps fittingly, Amiables like Jimmy Fallon make great talk show hosts: they are naturally agreeable with anything their guests happen to say. On the other hand, an Analytical like Dennis Miller, a very successful comedian who once tried hosting his own talk show gig, bombed big time.

A challenge of being with an Amiable is that, if you're more carefree socially and not as concerned about fitting in and going along with the crowd, the Amiable will be very upset, embarrassed, and nervous around you. Therefore, if you are an Expressive or Driver, remember that you can drive your Amiable mate to a high anxiety breakdown. He or she is trying so much to go along with you for the ride, but they need things to go smoothly. So, give in a little, consider their perspective, and you will do better with your Amiable mate.

Your Choice: Shopping or Visiting Your Mother-in-law?

Often, Amiables are viewed as aloof or shy. That is primarily because they do not want to say anything that might be inappropriate or embarrass themselves or others. Only when you get to know them and they feel comfortable with you, do their true feelings surface. However, if you are accustomed to being around Expressives or Drivers, moving to an Amiable can be a social shock. It may even drive you crazy.

In my case, I was married to a pure Expressive for more than 20 years. Then I fell madly in love with an Amiable (yes—after I divorced). One of the things I had to adjust to was a different mode of responsiveness from my partner. The Expressive partner would respond to anything I said, did, or even wear, with immediacy and passion of opinion, whether positive or negative. I became accustomed to such immediate and direct feedback. Yes, this could result in angst and ill-feeling, and lots of fighting, but I knew exactly where she stood on an issue. And then, with my new love, an Amiable, it was so completely different. Some of the times I didn't know whether she even liked me or liked doing what I suggested.

In all good relationships, many of the things we do have the intention of pleasing our mates. But if the other person is not responsive, it can be frustrating and create insecure feelings in ourselves because we are not sure of being on the right track.

A tip for those of you who may feel some of this frustration with your Amiable lover: give them choices. Instead of asking them what type of food they are in the mood for, ask them: "Which would you prefer Mexican or Italian tonight?" If you want feedback on what you'll wear to tonight's party, don't ask how you look in the blue dress, but rather: "Do you like the red or blue dress better?" And for vacation, the question should be structured as: "Would you rather go to Florida or New England or Europe for vacation?"

In this way, the Amiable knows that whatever their response is, it will probably be in the realm of something you already approve, and therefore, they can be assured that you are happy with their decision.

Sell to and Marry an Amiable

Salesmen love to sell to Expressives. You know the old saying: people in sales are suckers to other salesmen. But they love to sell to Amiables even more. Amiables can be persuaded. It drives me crazy when a couple comes into my office and one of them, usually the Amiable, is being taken advantage of by their partner. I've often seen Amiables stay in miserable relationships because they believe they can change their partner, or they have no choices, or they spend their time and effort trying to heal the effects of what is wrong.

An Amiable would never be sufficient for Hillary because he would not be able to contribute enough to her mission. On the other hand, I know a three-star general who does well with his Amiable partner, because he has no expectation of her in reaching his goals, except to be a loyal army wife.

If you are an Amiable, be careful. Expressives love the ready audience that you provide, and they can easily control you. You won't change over the course of your relationship, and they won't change.

Love is Lovelier the Second Time Around

Most often, the best mate for an Amiable is an Analytical. An Amiable wants to be very careful in their decisions to avoid upsetting their partner, while the Analytical wants to similarly evaluate decisions very carefully. Once together, they lead a nice quiet life, deliberating over decisions and carefully planning which car they'll buy, where to go on vacation, and how much life insurance they need. These couples are the ones with the big 401K accounts, but probably don't live in Palm Beach.

After reading this, one would think that Amiables would instinctively know to date somebody more like an Analytical, right? Wrong. To the contrary, they are mesmerized by all the wonderful things that Drivers and Expressives are going to bring to them. They're no different than the rest of us: they believe they'll be bored with Analyticals and other Amiables. After all, the Expressives are so much fun and charismatic (Bill Clinton). And, Drivers promise financial success (Donald Trump). Amiables consciously or subconsciously believe that they're chance for social or financial achievement may be hampered by their own personality style. They think, "If I can marry the achievement-oriented attorney, or the fun-loving car salesman, they can compensate for my _____ (Fill in the blank: shyness, unassertiveness, lack of drive). Then, I can be there to take care of him or her." Add to this thought process the idea that the Amiable believes they can help their partner eradicate obvious weaknesses, like flirting with coworkers or overdrinking.

> *The reason Amiables usually don't end up with other Amiables: They are swallowed up by Expressives and Drivers.*

We Drivers and Expressives are like vultures in going after the Amiables. We want an audience, we want someone to control and we can pick them out of a crowd almost instantly. And you Amiables are not blameless. You already realize that you have difficulty being assertive and motivated, you are attracted to the person who *will* be assertive, who will stand *out* in the crowd. Admit it—you let yourself fall into those relationships and are lead along for the rest of your time with him or her.

You Expressives and Drivers out there are already aware of Amiables. Amiables are a great audience and willing companion for you. I'm talking to you Amiables out there: Be careful of people with other personality styles and stand your ground. Convey to these people where you draw your boundaries and stick to it. For example, if you tell your Expressive boyfriend that he must be home by 7 o'clock because that is when the meal will be ready, stick to it. If he wanders in at 7:30, kick him in the ass, throw the spoiled dinner in the trash and demand that he take you to a nice restaurant. Wake them up to the premise that you will not be a pushover for their taking advantage of you. If they show that they can live with your rules, the relationship may work. If he or she ignores your requests and ideas, you'll have a miserable life. Move on to someone else who will respect your point of view.

Unfortunately, Amiables, more than other personality styles, are subject to abuse from their lovers. Draw boundaries, and if these boundaries are overstepped by the other, get out. If your spouse is demonstrating some kind of abuse, such as alcoholism or child cruelty, stand your ground, tell them that they must get professional help by a designated date, such as November 1st or December 31st. If they don't, leave.

Unconditional Love Sucks!

Leaving is the hardest thing for an Amiable, because they want to stay and nurture, please, and protect—or feel protected. As we have seen by now, it is their nature. The other person in the relationship intuitively knows this and they take advantage of it.

Too often, Amiables fail on the first go-around of a long-term relationship. As a result, they probably end up in divorce court even more than those wild and crazy Expressives. There is hope, however. I see many Amiables in successful long-term relationships the second—or third—time around. They have consciously or subconsciously told themselves, "I'm mad as hell and I'm not going to take it anymore!"

Fill in the blank. Three Amiable personalities you know:

_____
_____
_____

Now think: Hypothetically, could you stand to be married to them? And, if you have/had a child, would you be happy if your child were married to them?

KNOW IF AN AMIABLE IS THE ONE FOR YOU:

Their Plusses:
1. Easy to get along with
2. Good audience for others
3. Great in bed, once comfortable
4. Good planner
5. Creative

Their Minuses
1. Often lack self-confidence
2. Slow decision makers
3. Overly cautious
4. Difficult to read their feelings
5. Not the most fun musician in the band

Chapter 11
Detecting Personality Styles Outside the Bedroom

Hamlet: *"Though this be madness, yet there is method in it."*
—William Shakespeare

Maybe My Heart is Pure, But that's About It

Brain teaser: What do George Washington and Britney Spears have in common? The answer: almost 100% pureness. That is, pureness of personality style.

I already told you Washington was a Driver's Driver. Similarly, Britney Spears is about as Expressive as any public figure I've ever observed. She's been married three times, including once for only 55 hours. Talk about conditional love! She lost custody of her two sons several years ago (has now regained 50/50 guardianship) and even lost legal control of her own personal management for almost 15 years to her father. When she finally regained her legal freedom, she celebrated by posing nude on a beach. Now that's an expressive!

Purebred George

Just as purity is rarely found among politicians, fortunately for most of us, it is rarely found in personality profiles either.

Why is this so important? Because, as we meet, date, and cohabitate with lovers, we're not going to see black and white personality styles. Unlike the pure style evoked by Washington, most people we meet are blends and we may not be able to easily decipher their Driver-Analytical-Expressive-Amiable DNA.

But try anyway. Even if you identify a dominant and secondary category, you will have gone a long way in sizing up what you are in for.

Are You a Personality Star?—Probably Not

We've spoken about various presidents, but have not discussed Barack Obama. Where would you place his personality profile?

At first glance, he could fit an Analytical profile by his thoughtful, deliberate, and often prolonged decision-making process. Also, one of President Obama's best-known books, *Dreams From My Father*, is a very analytical self-evaluation about finding his identity. Contrast this approach to the best seller, Pulitzer-prize winning book by the late President Kennedy, *Profiles in Courage*, in which JFK did less analysis, but more description of historical people and their actions. So, we can check the Analytical box for Barack.

However, his willingness to please others around him indicates a strong leaning toward Amiable. Why, he even won the Nobel Peace Prize in 2009, his first year in office, pretty much before he had time to sneeze, let alone bring peace to the world. But many believe he deserved it because of the overwhelming feeling he generated that we should all just "get along with each other." If that's not an Amiable speaking, I don't know what is. Check this box, too.

Is he an Expressive? He clearly has some Expressive personality characteristics. He is better at telling jokes than many comedians, certainly fun at social gatherings, and has enough charisma to melt a rock.

So far, we've checked three personality boxes for this guy.

Well, if he is part Analytical, part Amiable and part Expressive, can he possibly be part Driver, too? Answer: One does not reach the office of presidency, with all the required organization, fund raising, and focus of mission, without being a Driver.

Regardless of what you may think of him politically, understand that Obama is a personality star, and he is a star because of his ability to exhibit and possess each of the four personality traits effectively. Who are some other all-around personality stars? Think about how these people have effectively used each of the personality traits:

- Benjamin Franklin
- Abraham Lincoln
- Ronald Reagan
- Ellen DeGeneres
- My chiropractor

My chiropractor, a star? Absolutely. Like most doctors, he has a good analytical perspective to scientifically evaluate patient solutions. But he also can relate to patients as well as Bill Clinton, the Expressive, who convincingly tells his constituents he "feels their pain." I've also seen my chiropractor very deferential to family and friends' wants, demonstrating his very Amiable traits. And his Driver side? Even though his office is cheerful and fun, it is managed better than a Disney theme park. As a result, this star doctor has been very successful financially.

Do you know any stars? Are you one? Maybe. The problem, however: When we are in the throes of infatuation, we naturally think our new lover is a personality star shining into our eyes. Think twice and be careful. After all, how many Ben Franklins are there?

But eHarmony Says We're Very . . . Harmonious

Evaluating mixed personality traits is especially important if you do online dating. Pew Research Center, in a 2015 survey, reports that 30% of all adults have used online dating sites. According to eHarmony.com, it's more than 40%, and that half of the 40% lie about three basic facts: age, weight, and income. No surprise there, especially if you know some of my friends who use the site.

But it's not really the lies (fibs?) that are the problem. What these sites really lack is knowledge about the person's <u>expected behavior</u>.

The problem with internet dating profiles is that people tell what they like to do, such as play tennis or travel to Europe, or walk on the beach at sunset, but they don't reveal how they *behave* when they do these things.

To illustrate, many of us in our profiles write that we would like to find a mate who also adores romantic walks on the beach, hand in hand, watching the sun slip gently behind the ocean's edge. But, let's ask ourselves: Who the hell is walking with us?

A walk on the beach with an Analytical will bring a conversation surrounding every detail of a new phone he just purchased, or her estimating what percentage of sunbathers are wearing bikinis. However, if you take a walk with a Driver—if he even has time for such a meaningless activity—he'll probably be looking at his watch to make sure that you don't miss the restaurant reservation in order to get the early bird special. On the other hand, an Amiable will be worried about being late for the reservation, too, but only because he does not want to upset the maître'd and cause a scene. Finally, if you happen to be with an Expressive, he hasn't even thought about dinner yet—you'll probably arrive a little late because they've spent too much time talking about themselves. And although the Expressive enjoys living in the moment, ironically, they may not even notice the sun at all.

There you have it. All four people indicated on the website that they like to take walks on the beach, But each walk is an entirely different experience for you, the person holding their hand.

Matchmaker, Matchmaker, Make Me a Millionaire Match

In the last several years, I've seen a lot of high-priced matchmaking companies that bring together upper level professionals. Besides a first date or a lunch meeting, customers can pay a lot of money to go to a cocktail party to mingle with other similar singles. Doctors, lawyers, and business owners will meet and mingle with each other for prospective dates. Unfortunately, this type of interaction ignores how people behave. As I said before, if you are a Driver CEO, unless your goals and focus are exactly the same as another Driver CEO, or Driver lawyer, etc., you will have frustration—and never know why. Indeed, the wealthy CEO may have more relationship success seeking out an Amiable who can agreeably help their Driver mate to stay focused on mission. Similarly, the successful Analytical architect may want to forget about finding a doctor, another Analytical, to hook-up with, but instead seek out

Unconditional Love Sucks!

a less-educated Expressive who can add light zest to his or her life.

Baby Apples Don't Fall Far from Daddy & Mommy Apples

I spent a great deal of time in Chapter 4 talking about evaluating parents in order to understand your partner. In keeping with the theme of inherited traits, you will see that personality styles pass down to children, also. Whether it's genetic or the environment, nurture or nature, I've consistently seen, for instance, parents who were predominantly Drivers have Driver offspring. And, the same for Analyticals, Expressives, and Amiables.

As a result of this tendency, you have one more avenue to predict how it will be with the lover you may be stuck with for what you hope to be the rest of your life—or at least the vacation you're planning together. If you are too blinded by love or their status or wavy blonde hair, and you are unable to decipher your partner's personality style, perhaps you can more clearly figure out the variety of tree that produced the apple.

For instance, if you are always falling for the quiet Analytical, do you think the child of Kim Kardashian would most likely fall into this category? What about the analytical propensity of the child of Apple co-founder and tech whiz Steve Wozniak, the brains behind the company's first computer? Here's a tougher one: the child of Wozniak's brash partner, Steve Jobs. What personality styles will she inherit? Here's a really tough one: the daughters of Elon Musk? Do you think they will have a higher chance of being an Analytical than the child of Kim Kardashian?

The Addicted Personality Style

Surrounding the four personality traits is the proverbial elephant in the room: the addicted personality. Addiction is an equal opportunity predator, conquering Drivers, Analyticals, Expressives, and Amiables. And just as we're unconditionally stuck with these four traits in people, we're too often connected to partners shackled by addictive behaviors: alcohol consumption, drugs, gambling, and sex, to name just the headliners. As one friend tried to explain to me, "I do everything to the extreme, and I just can't stop." He was a gambling addict on oxygen dying from COPD caused by an intense smoking habit.

Let's spend a few minutes talking about people who get tied in a relationship with the disease of alcoholism. This is a fascinating area because in my experience, alcoholics and substance abusers cover all four personality quadrants. According to a study published in the journal *JAMA Psychiatry*, nearly 30% of our adult population have suffered an "alcohol-use disorder." That means that there is almost a one-in-three chance that you or someone you meet has been there or is still there. I've seen people in all those quadrants fall for people with substance abuse problems. Some of these couples have had long, if not troubled, relationships which I even hesitate to state, because if you learn that others have endured through such relationships, you may think that you, too, can endure such a relationship. If you think you can, be prepared to endure.

Alcoholism and drug abuse are life-long diseases. Some victims are able to dry out, but most are not. According to a 2011 government study by the Substance Abuse and Mental Health Services Administration, less than 10% with alcohol dependence recognized the need for treatment, essentially confirming they are in denial. Chances are, therefore, if you are dating someone with a drinking problem, they are probably in the 90% group. Not good news.

I think the reason that *partners* of addicts fall into each of the personality profiles is because they attempt to address their problem from their own perspective. The Driver believes that they can change their partner because of the Driver's raw will to control the situation around them. The Amiable thinks they can tolerate the problem by going along with the flow, and then perhaps in time the alcoholic will see the light and initiate their own change. The Analytical thinks that as a result of their figuring out what exactly is wrong, they will eventually be able to tweak the problem back into alignment and live happily ever after. (Remember the Marilyn Monroe and Arthur Miller story in Chapter 10.) Finally, the reaction of the Expressive living with an addict varies. They may passionately and fervently attack the problem to get the person help, or they may almost ignore it and just walk away.

Many times, we stay with an untreated addicted person for reasons other than unconditional love. We may say to ourselves, either consciously or subconsciously, "I know they're an alcoholic, but they earn $385,000 per year and we have kids to raise." Or, "I know they have a drug problem, but I am not as young as I used to be, and I do not want to be alone." Or finally, "I believe they will eventually seek treatment and get better."

> *Unfortunately, these types of factors also play a major role in the people we fall for, even when they are not pot heads. Often, we don't look at the other person as much as we secretly evaluate what benefits could possibly arise from a relationship with them.*

Turning the tables, let's look at the relationship from the point of view of the unmanaged addict. Most abusers are functioning citizens and do not really want to change or give up their habit. My advice: grab an Amiable. They will tolerate and tolerate and then tolerate your behavior some more. If you come home late from having some drinks, they'll be upset but put up with it. If you get fired at work, they'll help you type up resumes for a new job. If you get a DUI, they'll help you find an attorney. They just want to get along and cope with the miserable situation in which they find themselves. Unfortunately, in order to please you, they will often end up drinking with you and may get hooked themselves.

Are you listening, all you Amiables out there?

On the other hand, if you have a substance problem and you really want to get dry, find a Driver. They won't put up with your shit. They will either get you to dry out, leave you, or kill you.

If you happen to have an addiction problem, and you are an Expressive, and a happy one, you'll probably end up dating a lot of other Expressives because Expressives love to have a good time, like you! No, there will not be a happy ending. Think Whitney Houston and Bobby Brown. Think Elvis and band buddies. And if you're too old for those notables, remember when Lindsay Lohan dated fellow rehab patient and snowboarder Riley Giles. Probably not a great idea.

To determine if you are dealing with someone who has addiction problems, visit the websites of treatment centers, such as Hazeldenbettyford.org or alcoholicsanonymous.com. They have lists

that describe typical symptoms. Here's my abbreviated list of how you can tell if the person you are falling in love with has a problem. He or she:
1. Needs a drink or drug to be more social or to have fun.
2. Always seems to have a drink in hand.
3. Is still drinking until it's time to (choose one): go to bed, or go home, or go to work, or throw-up, or, _____ fill-in-the-blank. Only when they have no choice but to stop drinking—like having to get on a plane, do they stop. Typically, others have stopped drinking earlier; they're still going.
4. Has had a DUI or auto accident or physical mishap (e.g., falling down stairs) while intoxicated.
5. As the day goes on, the drinks get stronger, say from beer to martinis.

Entirely switching gears now.

Which Bird Cage Do You Live In?

If you are gay and reading this book, you, too, should have figured out by now that your sexual orientation does not exempt you from the four personality profiles. The stereotypical flamboyant flamer one sees in the movies—think *The Bird Cage* and the character of Albert, played by Nathan Lane—may fit the style of an Expressive, but I know just as many Analyticals, Amiables, and Drivers who happen to be gay. One I know is a classic Analytical who is content to work with numbers all day and wouldn't be caught dead anywhere near a dance floor. Another I know is such a bottom–line Driver that he didn't even show up to his own birthday party because he could not break himself away from his busy office, well into the evening.

Just for the fun of it, what personality profile was Nathan Lane's partner in the movie, played by Robin Williams? My estimate: a Driver. Remember, his character, Armand, was so determined to solve his son's new fiancé problem, he even resorted to the extreme measure of recruiting his son's long-lost mother. It also fits that Armand managed their nightclub business.

Unconditional Love Sucks!

Successful Expressive and Driver?

Gay or straight, minority or not, there really isn't anything in this book that cannot be used by any "group," whatever your orientation, religion, or income level, especially with regard to my rules on marriage and unconditional love. By now, you have also seen that personality profiles cross the political and business spectrum as well.

Personality Styles Summed Up

In the end, you may be feeling a bit depressed, especially if you have categorized yourself in one of the quadrants, and you're focusing on the negative aspects. As a Driver, you may be worried that you come across as a sledge hammer to people. As an Expressive, you may have self-doubt about your self-control. If you're an Analytical, you may begin to think, if you haven't already, about how tedious you can be. And of course, for the Amiables—I say, of course, because the Amiables have already been worrying about their impression on others—you are worried about whether you can be assertive enough in order to avoid being a pushover.

I think the take-away of this section, besides evaluating the profile of the people you're dealing with, is to become aware that you must work on your weaknesses. And you have to work on bringing your best game to your relationships. So, if you are an Amiable, you should work on being more assertive. If you are an Expressive, work on planning your life a little better and not just doing things impulsively. For Drivers, learn a few jokes you can practice at the upcoming office party. And, of course, for analyticals, surprise your mate—and yourself—by doing some spur-of-the-moment things, the more dramatic the better. "Honey, we're going to Vegas this weekend, and we'll find a hotel when we get there."

Know yourself so you can improve yourself. Know others so that you can predict their behavior.

I like the layout of the chart to the right because it shows what profiles are typically on opposite ends of the scale and what profiles may overlap. The profiles in opposition, Amiable-Driver and Expressive-Analytical, are also the least likely to have success as couples in the long-term. Add to this list: Expressive-Expressive (Brad and Angelina) and Driver-Driver (Donald and Hillary).

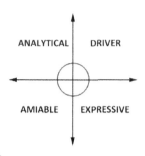

Notwithstanding the new wisdom you have just received, I have no false expectations. Yes, I am confident that within five minutes of meeting that blind date on a Saturday night, you will be able to deftly decipher their dominant personality style. But I am also confident that you may probably disregard negative traits you would normally reject if other characteristics of the person meet some of your dream objectives—and what I termed earlier Expectation Illusions. Things like killer good looks, a McMansion in the suburbs, or lots of income.

Look at the charts I have in Chapter 10 that summarize the positives and negatives of each personality style. Then, when you are dating or searching for someone, and you have figured out their dominant style, review the listed negatives. Can you tolerate those negatives? If you are Hillary Clinton, while you are working on accomplishing your mission, can you tolerate that Bill is going to screw around? If you are Melania Trump, can you deal with Donald's never-ending confrontations as he attempts to conquer the world?

It's not only tolerating Expressives and Drivers. If you fall for that successful—or not so successful—Analytical, let's say a software engineer—can you put up with the tedium of constant evaluation and data that leaves you screaming, "Just buy the stupid Honda! I don't give a shit how its mileage at sea level is compared to 19 other cars. It's my favorite color and I want it!"

If you love an Amiable, look at their negatives, too. They may be hard to read, a little boring, and not responsive enough for what you need. Can you live with that?

Two Negatives Do Not Equal a Positive

Don't fool yourself into thinking that you can keep the positives while changing the negatives in your partner. Unfortunately, the negatives come with the positives. It's a package deal.

Having read about the four major personality styles, you should practice categorizing friends and relatives—without disclosing what you're doing, of course. Which group do you find it easiest to get along with? Which type is most comfortable to hang out with and most satisfying for you? And which type do you find to be the biggest pain in the ass?

Use this information to evaluate which personality style could suit you best romantically. Although I spend the first part of this book talking about how dangerous UL is, I am also warning you to be prepared to live with the *personality styles* of your partner . . . unconditionally.

J. A. Dougherty

Part Four

THE LEGAL FRAMEWORK FOR ROMANCE – IN A CONDITIONAL WORLD

J. A. Dougherty

Chapter 12
Divorce: A Beginning, Not an Ending

"The biggest reason for divorce is marriage."
—Gene Simmons, of Rock Group *Kiss*

If there are many myths about marriage, there are even more myths about divorce. By now, you know the conventional statistic that reports a divorce rate between 40 and 50%. So, if it's happened to you, you share a common experience with almost half of all who have been married. However, if you haven't suffered through a divorce, a really bad break-up, or the death of your partner, this chapter may not apply to you, and I will not be offended if you skip it. However, you may still want to read the section on internet dating tips.

This chapter is not going to delve into legal strategies of the divorce process, or even why it happened. We know why it happened: Because UNCONDITIONAL LOVE SUCKS!

Instead, we will talk about discarding and rebuilding.

Grief Time

First, discarding. They say getting divorced is close to having your spouse or someone else in your family die. It really is like having a death in the family. In death, a loved one has left you and this is no different with divorce. Life without your partner means the end of an era – a major phase or period in your life, and it will never be the same again. That's why this chapter includes death as well as divorce from a mate.

This end of an era is why death is so traumatic. I will never be able to talk to my mother again about a favorite television show we shared. If I run into an old friend of my late father, I will not be able to call my dad and tell him about it. Similarly, if there is an old movie I used to watch with my spouse, I won't—and probably shouldn't—call him up and let him know.

After the long painful struggle of my own divorce, I didn't go out and celebrate with friends. I didn't take a Caribbean cruise. Instead, I just wanted to be alone and have quiet. I actually went for a long bike ride in the country. Perhaps it represented traveling to a new period in my life.

Yes, my grief started even before the judge issued the final decree. I would just sit, gazing out a window, or pretend to be watching TV with a blank stare. Work was even worse. Many say it's good to get through a grieving process by keeping busy at work. You may be different, but to that, I say, "Bull." I did not want to be there, and I was not very productive.

Of the many clients I've seen go through a big break-up, this hurt is normal. Pain is OK. And of course, I'm just a financial shrink, but you really may not need tranquilizers or antidepressants to fight the sadness. Let the sadness be there and allow yourself to wallow in it—for a while.

For those of you who divorced because of finding a new love, you may also feel some guilt and grief. But also, be grateful for your new situation, and do not dwell on what your ex may be going through. However, also be respectful of the grief of your ex and don't scold him or her for some of his grieving behavior. Have patience with him—and tell him to read this book!

Before my mother died, I would listen to Bruno Mars endlessly and sing along to his songs while driving, even as people drove by me looking curiously amused at my bouncy gestures. However, for some reason, during an extended time after my mother died, I just didn't have something in me to listen to my favorite singer. I can't explain it. But I also can't explain why after about 8 months, I began to gradually play his songs again. And now, a few years later, once again you can see me singing *Uptown Funk* at frequent intersections waiting for the light to change.

Don't Do Any Big Financial Moves

Especially from what you just read, you can see that this is a very vulnerable time in your life, and perhaps the most vulnerable. It's different from suffering dementia, but the results may be the same: bad decisions.

I usually advise my clients to make as few financial and life-changing moves as possible in the 12 months following a death or big breakup from a long-term or live-in relationship.

This includes being careful about changing jobs and houses or moving to another geographic area. Just let your life settle down. In many cases, because you both owned the same house, you may have to sell a jointly owned property or otherwise vacate your former residence. If so, it is no big deal to rent a place until you get more of your bearing. Living in a temporary abode for a year will allow you to figure out where and what type of place you want. During my divorce, I lived with my parents, and then several months later, I discovered I wanted to live by the coast. I eventually bought a house fifty yards from the ocean. Yay! But if I had rushed my decision, I would not have the gem of a place I have now.

Big no-no: Do not live with your ex-spouse after the divorce. I know this sounds impossible to contemplate but believe me, I've seen it, and it never ends well–even resulting in a visit by the police to break up a fight—your fight. You need your own place. Remember, you are starting over. And believe it or not, if love is to be rekindled with your ex-lover, there is a better chance of it if you live apart rather than together during this turbulent period.

One of the financial things you *should* do, however, is to change your will, your trust, the owners of your bank accounts, and the beneficiaries of your 401K and IRAs, to remove your ex-partner. If you suddenly die after your divorce and your nasty ex ends up inheriting all your money, you'd be so upset, that you'd probably want to kill yourself.

One of the financial things you should *not* do, is make impulsive investments. These include moving money out of one investment that you've been comfortable with to another, despite what your insurance salesman or brother-in-law says, or, buying that expensive timeshare because you've always wanted to vacation near Disney. Or worse, you buy the timeshare because you think your ex will find out and be jealous or envious—you hope.

Friends Will Often Try to Hook You Up

Once you're free of your former lover, watch out for the friends who care about you and want to help you by setting up blind dates or dinner parties with their available friends or cousins. Yes, they want to make sure you can get back into circulation, but too often, they want to help the other person just as much. Unfortunately, this other person is probably not your ideal partner, and you probably can't tell if they are or aren't, anyway, because you are still going through recovery from the most recent lover.

This can be a dangerous period for you because you may want someone to hang out with a little bit and have someone to make you feel whole again. Be careful, however, of compromising whom you settle for. You may tell yourself that you are just friends, but the other person may want much more. Then, before you know it, you are in a complicated situation at a time when you are trying to uncomplicate your life.

Another reason your friends may want you to get back into circulation prematurely is that social groups tend to be couples or singles. By that I mean couples tend to hang with other couples and singles with other singles. So now, if you're suddenly single because of a partner loss, it may be odd being the third—or fifth or seventh—wheel in your group of couples friends that you and your ex socialized with. I've seen singles that have had friends for years drift apart because of this strange phenomenon that makes no logical sense, but happens nonetheless. And there's another dimension to this: Now that you're single, one of your friends in the doubles group may be on guard about your stealing their own partner. Their mission is to keep you away from their Jim or Bob. I've seen this with friends who are in their thirties as well as their seventies.

When meeting friends of friends for blind dates or social occasions, tell them upfront that you are going through a recovery and taking it slow. And tell yourself, too, the same thing and believe it. Yes, as much as it may be tempting to jump into the sack with that new hunk you met at tonight's office party, slow down, and as the grief lessens, gradually begin to enjoy your new life.

The Same Old Patterns of Attraction?

You've heard it before: We tend to date or be attracted to the same type of person—over and over again. Now that you've survived the breakup, slap yourself on the side of the head and ask yourself—no, tell yourself—that this time can and will be different. The world is your oyster and there are lots of oysters out there. After reading about personality profiles in chapters 10 and 11, you should be more alert to the type you may tend to fall for and fall over.

And don't fall for the rebound relationship. If you were not able to change an abusive jerk or womanizer from the previous relationship, you probably won't with your new romance, either.

Recent statistics show that second marriages have a higher divorce rate than the first try, approximately 60%. Don't be discouraged, but don't be impatient, either.

Second marriages can be more complicated because we bring more of life's negative baggage to the relationship. Baggage may include children from prior relationships, money issues, relationship scars, and possibly still having to deal with ex issues. If necessary, spend a few dollars on a couple of counseling sessions to talk through and receive confirmation that you are on the right track going forward.

Leave as much of the baggage as possible behind you. You do this by not dwelling on old issues with your new partner. When chatting, talk about your future dreams and what you're going to do with the rest of your life. If they ask about your past, answer them with brief headlines about the issue, but then quickly change the subject to topics about looking ahead. Talk to your new partner about why the future is going to take you to fulfilling and exciting places, such as what hobbies or sports you're pursuing, how wonderful your job is, and perhaps what some of your travel plans will be, even if your new partner is not part of those plans. This approach is much more positive than always talking about how your last spouse cheated on you, or that your kids are losers, or that your boss is a witch. Don't be a Debbie Downer.

Internet Dating

As you embark on your new life, internet dating is almost an inevitability for many of us. Proceed but proceed with caution. The following tips are culled from shopping and lifestyle website mbgrelationships, and I think they're pretty good. Kelly Gonsalves is the contributing author.

1. Create an authentic profile.

When making your profile, showcase who you are and be upfront about what you're looking for from online dating. "Create an authentic profile that represents who you are as a person, the qualities you are seeking in a partner, and the type of relationship you ultimately want (e.g., marriage, short-term dating, etc.)," states Dr. Carla Manly, psychiatrist. An inauthentic profile may deter potential partners or, on the other hand, attract partners who aren't a good fit.

2. Don't lie about your age.

It may seem like a small fib, but lying about your age sets up any relationship you form on a foundation of dishonesty. When this person finds out your real age—and they will, eventually—it can feel like a massive betrayal of trust.

This also includes using up-to-date photos. "Take care that your photos represent you as you are now; avoid using photos taken more than two years ago," says Manly.

3. Take some good photos.

Speaking of photos, take some good ones if you don't have any already! "Make sure that your profile pictures represent you in a positive, upbeat way," Manly recommends. "No matter your age, a warm and smiling face is always inviting."

A few good rules of thumb are to take photos that are clear and high-quality (not blurry), without a lot of background clutter or other focal points (cats, children, etc.), she adds. *You* should be the focus of these photos.

4. Meet in person sooner rather than later.

"Although it's important to connect via messaging or phone until you feel comfortable, don't delay an in-person meeting for too long; what feels like a great connection online doesn't always translate into a great real-life fit," Manly says.

5. Be patient.

Just like good old-fashioned courtship from the days of yore, online dating takes time. It takes time to get your profile to a place that feels thorough and authentic, it takes time to get in the swing of online dating culture, and it takes time to find someone who you're interested in getting to know who's also interested in getting to know you. Not every interaction you have on a dating site or app will blow your socks off, and you're not going to feel sparks on every first date.

"Be patient and persevere," Manly says. "It's natural to find online dating a bit daunting, but there's a great deal of truth in the old axiom that you sometimes need to (metaphorically) kiss a lot of toads to find the right partner."

6. Enjoy the process.

You'll get the most out of your dating experience if you go in with an open mind and a light heart. There's so much joy, excitement, and curiosity to be had in getting to know an intriguing stranger and gallivanting about town for dates. Try not to put too much pressure on yourself (or anyone you meet), and enjoy the process. Even when you encounter people who are not the right fit, gracefully let them go, keep your head up, and keep it moving.

Stay Safe When Online Dating

Practicing online dating safety is vital for everyone but *especially* for those eagerly seeking love, who may be more likely to be targeted by scammers and frauds. While online dating scams can take many forms, one of the most common is someone matching with you with a very desirable profile, enthusiastically connecting with you, and then asking you for money in some way or form.

"Although some issues can be detected by staying aware, there are dating charlatans who are so practiced that it's difficult to detect their toxic ways early on," Manly notes. "If you get scammed, know that it's *not* your fault. Use the experience to improve your dating savviness."

Here are a few safety measures to adopt while online dating:

7. Never transfer money to someone you haven't met in person.

Many online dating scams involve getting you to send money to a person you think you're developing a romantic connection with. For example, a person you've been talking to from a dating site or app suddenly says they're having a financial emergency and asks if you can help them out by wiring them some money, putting money on a gift card, or sending some cash through Venmo or PayPal. Don't fall for it. If anyone asks you for money before you've even met in person, it's likely a scam.

8. Protect your personal and financial information.

Never share any personal information that can be used to access your finances or identity, such as your:

- Banking information
- Credit card information
- Social Security number
- Work or home address
- Last name
- Phone number

Yes, it's recommended to keep even your phone number private until you've met the person in real life or at least had a video call to confirm that they are who they say they are. Until then, keep communication only on the dating app or site where you originally connected.

9. Screen your matches carefully.

When you match with a new person on a dating site, Manly recommends screening their profile and messages very carefully. Scammers will often say they're currently traveling abroad or otherwise have a job that prevents them from meeting up with you in person, such as working on an oil rig, being in the military, or working for an international organization. They may also use disjointed language, answer questions vaguely, or have profiles on various dating sites under different names.

"Pay close attention to details that don't match up," Manly adds.

Unconditional Love Sucks!

"Don't hesitate to report any suspected fraud; customer service staff are generally very helpful and supportive, as they want to protect consumers."

10. Set up a video call or meet up early.

Try to meet up in person or at least hop on a video call sooner rather than later after matching with someone on a dating app. This way, you can make sure the photos match up to the person you're meeting in real life. If a person keeps avoiding meeting up with you in person and refuses video calls, that's a red flag.

11. Be wary of "love bombing."

<u>Love bombing</u> is when someone starts becoming way too romantic and affectionate with you way too soon. This is usually done to make you feel closer to them and make you more likely to acquiesce when they make requests for money or private information. Be wary if someone seems overly attached to you before they've even had a chance to meet you in person.

12. Meet up in public places.

You'll also want to keep safety in mind on any dates you go on from a dating app, but especially first dates. Manly recommends picking a public place such as a coffee shop, because these are generally safe and have other people in the vicinity.

13. Designate a safety buddy.

Manly recommends leaning on a trusted friend or family member who can help you vet profiles and people objectively. When you're going on a date, let this person know who you're meeting, when, and where, so they can keep tabs on you and make sure you get home safe.

Thank you, Kelly Gonsalves, and mbgrelationships for those great internet dating tips.

The Good News: Better Finances, New Beginnings, No Scars

There is lots of good news as you venture on to your new life after a break-up. The best news is that you now have total control of your life separately from anyone else. Perhaps for the first time in several years, you and you alone can freely decide:

- How to manage your finances,
- Where to spend your money,
- The type of car to drive,
- Whether to eat Chinese or have a pizza tonight,
- How much to put away in your 401K,
- The vacations you choose,
- Even where to live.

Contrary to conventional wisdom about being broke after divorce, you may have the opportunity to create more savings and financial wealth than ever before. I know this was certainly true in my case.

Don't believe the other convention that says all the good people are taken, so therefore you're out of luck in finding the good person for you. Nonsense. There's a he or she who is traveling through the same path of life experience as you. Maybe they've had a breakup or divorce. Maybe they've never looked hard enough for a partner. Perhaps their spouse passed away. There are good people out there. And you're a good person, too. Yes!

And, if you think you never ever want to get married again, have a glass of wine and read the next chapter. There is still hope!

Chapter 13
A New Framework:
The Promise Marriage

Dorothy: *"Toto, I have a feeling we're not in Kansas anymore."*
movie, *The Wizard of Oz*, 1939

These days, how are most couples avoiding divorce? By avoiding marriage.

Unless you've been living on the International Space Station for the last ten years, you know marriage has come under assault, and fewer people are doing it. Here are the reasons, summarized. You may have a few of your own that I've missed.

1. You went through a bad experience with a divorce of your own parents.
2. You can't find one who meets your expectations, i.e., you haven't fallen in love yet.
3. You fear that unconditional love is not realistic these days, given our culture of check-list dating.
4. You do not want to compromise your dedication to a career ladder.
5. You fear a loss of financial assets if later divorced.
6. You don't agree that a public contract—that is, legal marriage—should vouch for a personal and private love.

Here are a few demographic results from the widespread adoption of the views listed above:

1. The marriage rate is the lowest since they've been keeping records.
2. The U.S. birthrate is shrinking.
3. 40% of children born are to non-married parents.
4. World economic growth is affected. For instance, in Japan, more diapers are sold for senior citizens than for babies.

Young people are not getting married, let alone having children.
5. People are pessimistic that long-term happiness with another person is possible.

Notwithstanding these discouraging lists, surveys show that two people living together is good for everyone. Children are better off, the economy grows more, we live longer because someone is there to take care of us, and most important, we have someone to go to the movies with.

Obviously, something is happening. Have you ever asked yourself why *any* of us would want to get legally married, which binds us to IRS rules, state laws, lawyers, and accountants? Doesn't a marriage, after all, represent something very personal—the most personal thing in our lives? Yet, historically, most of us at one point in our life decide to say having this personal relationship isn't enough; we want to make it a legal connection. Indeed, most religions will not marry a couple unless there's a legal certificate involved.

In spite of our strong tradition of state-ordained marriage, cultural trends and legal considerations are making such a partnership much less frequent. The unfortunate result of these trends leaves the status of our committed romantic relationships whirling in the wind like a weather vane with no steady direction.

The Promise Marriage

What is the answer to this quandary in which we find ourselves? One answer is what I call the Promise Marriage. Some have called it a spiritual marriage, but it's really much more. A Promise Marriage consists of a public ceremony, like a wedding—perhaps with religious clergy, in which the couple makes a long-term commitment to each other before their friends, family, and children, if kids are already in the picture. Ideally, a Promise Marriage is also one in which both parties have read this book.

It is up to you and your partner whether to tell others that you decided not to stop by city hall for a license. As a result, nobody has to know, and, indeed, as we move into the future, more and more of us will care less and less about sanctioning the relationship.

Unconditional Love Sucks!

> *A Promise Marriage is much more than a spiritual marriage, which somehow relies on ethereal hopes of unconditionality. At the same time, a couple may include any and all religious rituals they wish in their ceremony.*

By promising to commit that each of you will bring your best to the relationship, each of you understand and acknowledge that unconditional love is a dangerous myth. And although we come to the relationship with personality traits and styles that we must accept going in, these traits are no excuse for *not* making our A-game effort to sustain a successful romance.

Benefits of Rings Without the Contractual Slings

There are several reasons a Promise Marriage may be a good solution for many couples:

1. Children have more domestic and familial security knowing that their parents are in a committed, long-term marriage.
2. Income, assets, and debt may continue to be managed separately, which is what I advocate for all couples.
3. If you don't tell people it's a non-licensed marriage, they won't ask.
4. You both know that you can not take anything for granted; you're with each other because you want to be, not because of a legal contract.
5. It eliminates the need for a pre-nuptial agreement. Only about 3% of marriages get a prenup, anyway.
6. You avoid various "marriage tax" penalties.

In addition, there are penalties that society imposes on legally married couples:

1. Credit "link" (the bad credit of one partner hurts the other)
2. Auto insurance "link" (rates for both go up if one is a bad driver)
3. Mortgage "link" (most spouses must be on the loan—

i.e., the hook)
4. Inability to have two taxable homestead properties
5. Possible loss of disability and Medicaid benefits
6. Medical cost liability "link" (partner becomes responsible for cost of other)

Also, be aware of the following:
- A prenuptial agreement may still be needed in common-law marriage states. Some of them have rules in place that determine how assets are to be allocated between partners in a break-up if there is no prior agreement.
- If one of the partners never works outside the home, having made less income than his or her mate, this person's surviving social security benefits at retirement age will be less than if legally married. This is much less of an issue, if any, with both partners working.
- Some states offer special asset-protection rules in lawsuits for legally married couples not available to other couples. I have seldom seen this rule come into play, however, and separate ownership of assets may more than offset the advantage that comes with legal marriage.
- Your pastor or rabbi may frown upon a Promise Marriage. This is a bit ironic since you would think their focus on personal spirituality and commitment overrides what civil lawmakers create. If this is a problem, find a new pastor.

Unconditional Love Sucks!

In an interview with Vanity Fair, celebrity Goldie Hawn detailed how avoiding legal marriage has kept her love partnership together. She said that she would have been "long divorced" if they had gotten married at City Hall. She believes that "there's something psychological about not being (legally) married because it gives you the freedom to make decisions one way or the other. For me, I chose to stay. Kurt (Russell) chose to stay, and we like the choice." At this writing, Kurt and Goldie have been together 40 years and are romantic partners in an industry of very competitive beautiful women and men. It is interesting that her word of choice to describe the relationship is "freedom."
(Vanity Fair, April 2017)

Goldie and Kurt: *Freedom to stay together*

Let's Increase the 40% Rate

In describing the Promise Marriage, I am not advocating a "single" status for parents. You tell your children that you are married. There are few things I feel more strongly about than children raised in a home with two parents committed to each other and committed to making a secure and comfortable home for the children they raise. You can emotionally and politically react negatively to this, and argue to the contrary, but statistics show this environment has the greatest chance for creating the most successful children. Nothing beats the feeling a child has when he can tell himself and the world around him that he has the love and continuity of two parents—parents who reinforce the idea that they will be there during good times and bad, happy and sad, to provide structure and even a slap on the ass from time to time.

But how that family unit is formed, and what the legal bounds are, will continue to change.

Statistics show that a marriage (straight or gay) is good for raising successful children. More than other arrangements, marriage provides a more stable household, it allows interaction with varied types of role models, and results in a higher feeling of security and love.

Studies have also shown that a secure upbringing leads to stability and success in adult life. More and more couples are considering a public partnership culminating in a wedding ceremony, but doing it without the marriage license, thereby not subjecting themselves to state law for something they view as a very personal situation outside the purview of the State. This trend may be partly the result of the growing economic and social power of the female partner, who, unlike a few generations ago, does not necessarily need or want the legal bonds to protect her social and financial interests. Another factor is that when once-divorced couples want to remarry, they often want to keep their assets separate. Yet they still want to consider themselves "married" and want to hold out to themselves, their children, and to the public that they are indeed married.

A Promise Marriage is certainly better than telling the children:

"Joe is your father, but we're not married because we are not willing to commit to each other." This statement implies that Joe could leave any day, and, "Hey kid, don't bother having the secure feeling that you will have two loving parents around for you." An analogy that may hit home: Let's pretend that auto engineers tell us that the brakes on our cars will work only about 50% of the time. Even though your car may be very comfortable to sit in and beautiful to look at, how does that knowledge of probable break failure affect the pleasure you have with your driving experience? Now you know how 40% of children feel about the domestic security of their childhood experience.

Bring Your "A" Game, Not Hidden Motives

If you think about it, a Promise Marriage—as opposed to a legal one—is one more way to encourage you to bring the best to your relationship. You can't take each other for granted simply because you have a paper license from the state that says you are stuck with each other—at least until you're legally divorced. You can't sit on the couch and dog it with the attitude that your husband or wife is legally bound to you. On the other hand, if you do not legally marry, then the other person does not have a legally binding reason to put up with your pigging out on potato chips and spilling beer on the new sofa.

Of course, if one spouse will greatly benefit financially from having a legal marriage, either through the sharing of assets, or perhaps the potential receipt of future alimony, you can be damn sure there will be a marriage license waiting at the altar. Do not expect your partner to be direct to you or even themselves in their motives about this. But if you bring the Promise Marriage issue up, listen closely to their reaction; it may be very revealing.

If your soul mate is not willing to marry in this manner, then are they truly worth marrying on a legal basis?

Several years ago, one couple I knew divorced for tax purposes, then remarried five years later. The IRS could probably have nullified the divorce for lack of substance and declared that they were still legally married—at least for tax purposes. However, the secret divorce went well until it was inadvertently revealed to the woman's mother—and their four kids! Under the new tax code, started in

2018, there are incentives once again for some very high-income couples to ditch the legal rings.

Legal Nuts & Bolts, Briefly—Very Briefly

When investigating common-law marriage laws in which a state classifies a domestic relationship as a legal marriage, to determine if they apply to you, be sure to include the name of the state with your internet search.

The ramifications of a break-up from legal marriage continue to evolve. More and more women have income that exceeds that of their husband. We have more stay-at-home dads, unemployed dads, parental house dads. Changing roles, and even recent changes in the tax code, are affecting divorce settlements. If you're a woman, do not take it for granted that you will be awarded full custody of children and related child support or alimony. Instead, you may have to pay it, and under those new tax laws, it will *not* be deductible. I believe this trend, along with the growing independence of financially successful females, will result in fewer and fewer legal marriages.

A non-licensed marriage brings to the forefront that the relationship is not based on unconditional love. In essence, you are both saying, "Since I have no legal bind to you, nor you to me, there is nothing keeping us together except our vows of commitment and the promises we made." These vows of commitment are to each other.

> *It is somewhat ironic that gays have recently won their legal right to marry while heterosexual marriage rates significantly decline. Notwithstanding new laws, most gay couples have not chosen the legal path, perhaps for the same reason others have not. There are many attractive tax and financial planning options when you are legally single, both for straight and gay. Check with a financial advisor to review your individual situation.*

If you are going to embark on a Promise Marriage, as opposed to a legal marriage, should you tell others? People will try to hold it out that you are really *not* committed to each other. Legal vs. not legal—it's none of their business. Don't tell your kids, your mother-in-law, even your boss. Have the wedding ceremony, and the guests will not tell the difference if you make it appear that way. It's none of their business whether it is legal or not.

Meet Mr. and Mrs. Smith

As word gets out about the Promise Marriage and other concepts introduced in this book, more couples may become comfortable telling others that their bond is not a traditional legal one. In the meantime, if you would rather the world not know, you have that right.

One lady I know changed her last name to that of her partner so that society would automatically assume there was a legal marriage. I was fooled on their first visit at my office to have a tax return prepared. When I asked the couple why they did not want to file a joint return, they politely objected, explaining they could not legally file jointly because there was no legal marriage. I, their discrete financial advisor, was the only one that knew this fact. The world knows them as Mr. and Mrs. Smith—no relation to Brad and Angelina.

When you go to the hospital and staff asks if you are partners, if you say yes, they will not do a records check with the county clerk. If booking a cruise, tell your travel agent you are travelling with your spouse. They won't care. These days, nobody seems to care! Probably because so few partners are legal spouses.

Most of the world will never know or care if you're legally married. However, lenders like to know if you are, so they can put each of you on the hook. For these situations, if not legally married, indicate that you are not and push to have just one of you sign on to the loan.

If you and your partner have committed to each other in a marriage ceremony with marital commitments in front of your friends and family, and you have chosen *not* to be bound by artificial state laws and rules—and divorce attorneys—then that is your decision and nobody else's business.

And if anyone questions you, tell them to ask Goldie and Kurt.

Chapter 14
Because I Want You

> Noah: *"So it's not going to be easy. It's going to be really hard. We're gonna' have to work at this every day, but I want to do that because I want you. I want all of you forever—you and me, every day."*
>
> —Movie, *The Notebook*, 2004

You may get the impression that the parting thought of what I want to leave with you is that all romantic relationships are predictable and essentially based on some kind of business-like list of conditions. Absolutely not. But in a sense, they are, because a legal marriage is a legal contract without a termination date until death or divorce. Perhaps this sense of locking in terms reduces romantic effort by partners.

I joke with my clients that politicians should re-write the marriage laws to have fixed-term contracts almost like a lease agreement. We could have, say, a five-year written contract, and at the end of the five years, if the love partners decide to part ways, they do just that, with all issues of asset division pre-agreed upon in the contract. Or, if they choose, they can renew for another five years with the same or modified terms. Right.

Of course, divorce attorneys would not like this arrangement.

Even if you are part of what I have termed a Promise Marriage, you may also end up creating some legal contracts and partnerships. If you have children or own property together, or if you have a joint bank account, or if you make financial promises or exchanges to each other, you could still have attorneys involved if you split up.

We have all heard the cases about the guy who gives his sweetheart an engagement ring and she breaks off with him. Is she obligated to return the ring? They were not married, but the conditional gift may be an implied contract. They will probably see each other again after all—in court.

My proposition is this: Look at your partnership as a business relationship and prepare for it initially as if it were a business relationship, then you can enjoy it as a romance. And even be surprised by the romance. Most couples naturally do it the other way around, to everyone's heartache. An example of taking care of business up front is the establishment of a prenuptial agreement. You may also need a prenuptial in states that recognize common-law marriages and relationships. Whether your marriage is sanctioned by the state or not, consider having a few "board" meetings at the kitchen table to discuss and agree on how bills will be paid, and assets arranged. I described this in Chapter 8.

Matchmaking, Reality TV Style

One of my favorite reality TV shows was *The Millionaire Matchmaker* with Patti Stanger. As the title suggests, rich singles come to Patti, often desperate to find their soul mate. Most are in their thirties or older. Even though they've conquered the professional world, they are at a loss to maintain a long-term romantic relationship. How on earth can that be? They're rich and often good looking and drive very sexy cars. What could possibly be the problem?

It soon becomes evident that their extreme personality makes them impossible to put up with. The Expressive is too unbearable, the Driver too obnoxious, the Analytical too tedious, and the Amiable—well, they don't even get to go on the show.

But here is the very compelling component of *The Millionaire Matchmaker* for me: It doesn't take Patti more than three minutes to observe these flaws in her client. We do, too. Then Patti, with great passion and directness, coaches the millionaire to smooth out their rough edges and to change their ways. If the client can simply do what Patti tells them to do, then their date—usually a person most of us would call a very good catch—will fall into their arms happily ever after. Easy, right?

Not a bit! The client, even after a few proverbial slaps from Patti, *cannot manage to alter their personality*. It's amazing to watch the client stuck in an unalterable version of themselves, even at the expense of turning off a very attractive mate—and simultaneously frustrating the hell out of the rest of us who are watching from our sofas at home.

Patti's clients provide a window in to all our relationships. And to ourselves. They remind us of three truths that I've tried to illustrate throughout these chapters.

1. Change is hard. Don't count on you or your lover changing over time, especially for the better.
2. Although our relationships are based on expressed or implied conditions, once we're with somebody, we must understand that a person's personality traits, summarized in the four styles I discussed, define their behavioral patterns that we must accept going into the deal. And this acceptance must be . . . unconditional.
3. Even if we think we are God's gift to love, or have tons of money and eventually exchange wedding rings, lovers and potential lovers will not be blind to our bad behavior—or other crap we hope they'll tolerate and tolerate unconditionally.

We Do Better the Second—or Third—Time

Think back, if you will, to the dinner party I described at the very beginning, in which all my companions believed in unconditional love, but all of them—all of us—had moved on to our second or third spouse. As I looked around the table during the discussion, I noted that the person formerly married to the out-of-control alcoholic had remarried one who is sober. The one with the cheating husband remarried one who was not prone to having affairs. And finally, the one who fell for the successful office coworker, eventually married someone who was, well, very successful.

As an observer, as well as participant, it was possible to see that in later relationships we did a better job in having our conditions satisfied, and also, and just as important, we paid more attention to make sure we satisfied the expectations of our new partners.

It was agreed by all around the table that we could—no, should—have done a better job at selecting our partner the first time around and also being better partners for them.

After more lighthearted reflection, the host poured another round of wine—and we talked away the evening and laughed at what life brought us.

Long-Term Love Is Possible, Even with Celebs

In Chapter 7, I mentioned the 50-year celebrity marriage of Joanne Woodward and the late Paul Newman. When asked how their marriage lasted so long, Newman reportedly answered, "People stay married because they want to, not because the doors are locked." That is a better definition of *conditional* love than I've ever heard. You have to *want* it to be successful—it doesn't happen unconditionally. Realize that the doors are never locked.

The Newman's—Very cool before and after pics—and smiling even more.

In the end, be smarter, be more romantic, and bring your best game, even when you think you shouldn't have to.

Take a Bath and Have Some Pizza

I love the story I heard about an old aunt who left a sealed gift box for her niece and the niece's husband, with the instruction that it was to be opened only if they got into the most horrible, unresolvable marital conflict. The box promised to hold the key for restoring romantic love and understanding. Over the years they had conflicts, of course, but before getting to the point of opening the box, they always ended up resolving the problem themselves, as if challenging themselves to solve their dilemma before resorting to the aunt's last hope. They told each other they never wanted to admit that they could not have an issue they couldn't resolve.

Then, after many years of successful marriage, they finally opened the box for the fun of it, merely out of curiosity to see what magical secret was in the box. After all those years of wondering, they simply found: First, a note that read, "Get some pizza," second, a 20-dollar bill for him, and, third, for her, a fancy soap bar, with one more note, "Enjoy a nice bath."

The point the sweet aunt was making: The box had more power closed than open. Twenty bucks and a bar of soap were not the issue. The mysterious bundle forced the couple to find reasons to keep loving each other, to bring the best in themselves to the relationship rather than relying on a complacent myth of unconditionality contained in a magic box.

And, if all that still doesn't work, well, that's what the pizza is for. After all, Darwin said it best: We're all just human.

An Important Request

Thanks for reading my book! I really appreciate all of your feedback, and I love hearing what you have to say.

I need your input to make the next version of this book—and my future books—better.

Please leave me a brief helpful review on Amazon letting me and others know what you thought of the book.

Thank you very much.

Thank You Notes

As with any project of time and effort, this project would not have come to light if not for several amazing people who I am lucky to have in my life.

Dawn Angier was kind enough to do all the editing of the text, tedious because of its nature, laborious because of the author's unpredictable proclivities. I also have her to thank for more than once honing me in on perspectives I had not considered in a project that at times probably has too many.

Michael Angier deserves unending thanks for doing all of the heavy lifting for the production of this book. An experienced author, editor, and life coach, he has certainly required all of these skills to get this project to completion. I have come to depend on Michael's experience and judgment in a myriad of aspects of my professional and now writing life, and for this I give many thanks.

Of course I cannot forget my clients. Over the years, so many have become my closest friends and companions. If I have referenced any of their experiences in this book, every effort has been made to disguise their true identities. During the journey of their lives and mine, I have enjoyed sharing the ride.

And I can never forget my lovely wife, Susan. From her I have learned much. Susan's patience, faith, and unending flexibility have truly allowed me to complete this project—with very few conditions indeed.

Photo Credits and Licenses

Blake Shelton with Miranda Lambert: S.Bukley/Shutterstock.com
Blake Shelton with Gwen Stefani: J.Seer/Shutterstock.com
Caitlyn Jenner: Featureflashphoto/Shutterstock.com
Stephen Paddock: Eric Paddock, picture on Twitter
Lisa Marie Presley: S.Bukley/Shutterstock.com
Donald & Melania Trump: /Shutterstock.com
Elliot Spitzer & Silda Wall Spitzer: Globe-Photos/ImageCollect
Kim Kardashian: /Shutterstock.com
Michael Jackson in concert: Jomic/Shutterstock.com
Michael Jackson with sunglasses: S.Moskowitz/GlobePhotos/ImageCollect
Ronald Grant Archive/Alamy Stock Photo
Woody Allen: MARKA/Alamy Stock Photo
Dwayne Johnson: Zuma Press/Alamy Stock Photo
Donald Trump: A.Katz/Shutterstock.com
Hillary Clinton: /Shutterstock.com
Rodney Dangerfield: Album/Alamy Stock Photo
Pres. Gerald Ford: Alamy Stock Photo
George Washington: /Shutterstock.com
Robin Williams & Nathan Lane, The Birdcage: Album/Alamy Stock Photo
Goldie Hawn & Kurt Russell: G.Fullner/Shutterstock.com
Paul Newman and Joanne Woodward (earlier): Globe Photos/ImageCollect
Paul Newman and Joanne Woodward (later): R.Makler/Globe Photos/ImageCollect

About the Author

J. A. Dougherty is a graduate of LaSalle University in Philadelphia and the Stern School at New York University. He resides in Florida where he continues his couple*s*—correct that, *financial*—counseling practice. His wife of 12 years continues to tolerate him—with some conditions, of course.

The author has hosted numerous radio shows and presented several seminars on wealth management.

Made in United States
North Haven, CT
03 May 2024